The Noisemakers:

Why They Keep Losing

Your Money and How to

Make It Stop

by Steve Orr

Printed in the United States of America by

Press On Publishers

Victoria, TX 77904

http://www.thenoisemakersbook.com

ISBN 978-0-9827672-2-1

19.95

Cover design by Rebecca Price

I have lived, Sir, a long time, and the longer I live,

the more convincing proofs I see of this truth-that

God governs in the affairs of men.

And if a sparrow cannot fall to the Ground

without His Notice, is it probable that an Empire

can rise without His Aid?"

~ Benjamin Franklin,

To Colleagues at the Constitutional Convention

CONTENTS

Freedom had been hunted round the globe;

reason was considered as rebellion;

and the slavery of fear had made men afraid to think.

But such is the irresistible nature of truth,

that all it asks, and all it wants, is the liberty of appearing.

~ Thomas Paine, Rights of Man, 1791

INTRODUCTION

A year ago I was thinking about how satisfying life could be. I started at pretty much the bottom in life like most folks, got a little lucky, worked hard and never let an opportunity pass me by. The result was that I had been in many businesses, progressed, learned, got into the financial business, drilled a few oil wells, learned to fly twin engine airplanes and captain big boats. Before I knew it we were quite comfortable and able to do things we never thought we would or could.

During my stints into business I developed niches and was creative enough to find ways to give myself an edge and invent new competitive ideas. I read as many books as I could to find out how the best performers did it and constantly tried to get to the next level. I started in the financial sector by working in the insurance industry selling life insurance through a fraternal company to Lutherans. All was great, but I am not a corporate guy and was not happy selling only five mutual funds when I knew there were thousands. I wanted to have the best, and if I was going to get them, my clients might as well have them too. I also wanted to be completely unbiased, have access to all types of investments and not be beholden to any corporation or have conflicts of interest.

Things were going good. We had a small but extremely profitable company and I could cruise to the end of my life making plenty of money, not having to retire. I had developed systems and products that I proved were superior to the normal brokerage or investment firm. I did this by not depending entirely on the stock and bond market. Early on, I discovered that it is better to have eight or nine different asset classes instead of the normal two.

I thought my systems and investments were good enough that if I wanted to expand I could grow a pretty substantial company. I even dabbled and went so far as to hire some folks to help explore the idea, but I always went back to just me and my administrative staff. Jeez, it was cutting into my fishing time for Pete's sake! Then came the crash. I was mad. The new people coming in my door had 20 to 80% less money. My clients fared much, much better. Then came a new administration and the only thing I could see was that things were getting worse, especially for the majority of the world who were dependent on only stocks and bonds. I'll explain later.

The dynamic had changed dramatically and I realized that the country could actually fail. My kids could be without opportunity. The darn cause had gotten bigger than me. Nuts! I've heard of this somewhere before. So, here I am writing this book so folks can understand how the system really works instead of what they are taught by the typical brokerage houses (wire houses) like Merrill Lynch, Edward Jones, Morgan Stanley, AG Edwards, Smith Barney, etc. etc. There are too many to name. These people look at you like prey: like a deer hunter looks at a deer, like a fisherman looks at a fish. They shoot or hook you, stuff you, put you on the wall for a while to show you off and then lock you in a box and put you in the back of the closet after you are no longer of any use to them.

New dynamics are evolving. When bad things happen, opportunities are created. We must stay on the cutting edge! You've heard it. Money can be made when blood is running on the streets. You just don't want it to be your blood that others are making money on! Money will be raised now in very different ways than it was before. Because of prohibitive regulation and a left wing and radical Congress and President, entrepreneurs and the wealthy are either heading for the proverbial hills or trying to figure out how to head for the hills. We now not only need to educate our citizens on the types of investments they will need, but on the rudimentary workings of a capitalistic society and why it is the only system that can work and how it is being subverted by the "Noisemakers" for their own gain and craving for power.

These "Noisemakers" have divided the country over the last 70 years or more so they could work their way into power. They have pitted conservatives against liberals, doctors against hospitals and insurance companies against drug companies. Blacks, Hispanics, whites, Asians and others are intentionally kept in a permanent "state of hate" regarding one another. In other words, everyone thinks the other guy is the bad guy. The noise is now a roar. It is about hate, revulsion and loathing. We are living in the midst of complete political polarization. They, the Noisemakers, simply must divide us in order to promote their agenda. Knowledge is their enemy. They consider capitalism and free enterprise the problem, even though a controlled economy similar to or the same as socialism has never worked and cannot. These Noisemakers take advantage of well-meaning people. By that, I mean that they either don't explain or don't themselves understand the consequences of their actions.

I see the Noisemakers as hunters. They are seriously stalking and seeking to destroy. They won't be happy until we are all shot and stuffed. They are the white noise of the world that drowns out meaningful dialogue and understanding between us. They are not who you think they are. They cannot allow the capitalist system to function properly. To take something over, you must first destroy what exists. They exploit and magnify, or even cause weaknesses in the system to promote their agenda. This is government as a negative and is good only for those in control. This causes an economic "death spiral." It is the actions of the Noisemakers which have caused the deep recession we are experiencing today.

Hence the book. We will explore the system and the people affecting it, including you, Joe and Jane Citizen. You will get to know me and I will hopefully provoke and promote thought. The goal of my classes, workshops, radio shows and writings is just to get people to think things through and eliminate the "noise." Stop listening to the language of the Noisemakers and THINK!! I am a solutions guy so I will give you my opinion of what I believe can be done.

A special note to my GenY readers: I know you have little patience with partisan garbage. I'm not just another blow-hard conservative, I'm a serious citizen. You may disagree with some of the things I have to say, but please keep reading. If you only take away the idea of civic participation or learn more about how to invest your money, so be it. Don't put this book down and walk away because my politics rub you the wrong way. I want us to sit at the table together and discuss and debate. That's why I've put my email address at the end of every chapter. Are you mad? Tell me about it. Think I'm crazy? Let me know!

This book will have solutions that will positively affect you where you live. Life is good: Puda Vida. And by the way, let's all make some money.

~ Steve Orr

If Virtue & Knowledge are diffused among the People,

they will never be enslav'd.

This will be their great Security.

~ Samuel Adams,

letter to James Warren, February 12, 1779

The Noisemakers Are Winning.

Are the Noisemakers Winning?

You Decide.

The US is such a vibrant country! Since first landing on the shores of this continent, we have invented, morphed, and developed into the most successful country the world has ever known. When our forefathers came here they were the entrepreneurs of the Old World. They were the liberty lovers; the folks who understood and felt the laws of nature that drive some to constantly innovate and reach for the stars in their endeavors. They walked across this vast land, fought it, survived it and built never before dreamed of wealth for themselves and their communities. It wasn't all peaches, cream and roses, but we made it in spite of some terrible mistakes. As we continue to move forward, we have to remember the natural laws and sins of human beings.

What matters is what systems work best to enable man to live within an environment and to constantly improve and progress. What systems allow the next generation to live in a better world with more opportunity than the previous generation? This is the tricky part. We know there are diametrically opposing views on how this can happen. Thus, we must explore together, using the laws of nature and human behavior, and systematically think through the processes and behaviors that allow man to achieve and improve so that our children have it better than we do. This is a country where a person like me, who was bored with school, did not conform to the norm, was, in fact, a complete rebel who got in lots of trouble, can still start at the bottom and get to the top. I have experience doing such things as scrubbing floors in airports, delivering newspapers, digging ditches in 30 degrees below zero between railroad tracks with a jackhammer, and working as an offshore oil rigger in the gulf in 120 degree heat generated by the summer sun on the deck of a steel barge.

I went on from these varied jobs to develop businesses. From selling life insurance, I moved into the financial industry, innovated and become what some would call "successful." As Napoleon Hill says in his book, *Think and Grow Rich*, "Success is the progressive realization of worthy ideals." Some say this can happen anywhere: I think not. I think that it can only happen in America. I am concerned that we Americans have been steadily losing the opportunity for success. I see us as a people speeding like a race car out of control. We are heading for the wall and about to crash. We have forgotten how to drive.

The United States has grown and evolved to the point where it is devouring itself, not unlike Europe, which has been doing it for quite awhile. I saw a show on TV recently where Oprah was in Denmark. She was talking with a young woman who was so happy with her life. She had free health care, and was looked after by the government. In fact, if she lost her job she would be paid 90% of her salary for four years by the government.

This is how the American entrepreneur would respond to such a government system: First they would work until they could qualify for the four-year vacation, take it and find a way to work also. It would be for cash so they wouldn't get caught and have to pay fines or penalties and the 75% tax imposed by the country. This is the entrepreneurship of the ghetto, i.e., manipulate and get all you can out of the system and get cash on the side. The poor as well as the rich in America have things. The problem is that much of their cash comes from illegal activity. If you over-regulate and try to snafu the American entrepreneur, they get mad, feel assaulted and their moral stance on life changes. They say, "If you're gonna stick it to me, I'm gonna stick it to you." I saw this very thing in the Overtown section of Miami where I built the cable TV system in the 1980's. These folks living in the ghetto on unemployment had rolls of cash and plenty of things.

What is the message to the youth here?

Upon analyzing the United States' great experiment with democracy and capitalism in the eighteenth century, Alexander Fraser Tytler commented, "Beware when the politicians can bribe the people with their own money."[1] He was betting that the experiment would fail when government got too big and interfered with both democracy and capitalism. Benjamin Franklin loved this quote. Why is big government so dangerous? Because, for starters, it's so hard to realize that you are losing your freedom when someone is putting a check in your hand. Most citizens of the United States don't connect the fact that the money in their hand, courtesy of this program or that program, is really their own money, minus taxes and administrative fees.

Who wouldn't vote for someone who gave him or her a "free" check? Would you vote for someone who would give you a bigger check the more children you bore? (That is, as long as they don't have a father present.) This is the welfare system. It creates incentives for people to manipulate the system, thereby trapping the unwary and giving them no incentive. For decades Americans have been saying that this sort of welfare system is bad and needs to stop, but it doesn't. Do you know why? It is a perfect vehicle to allow the Noisemakers to achieve their goal of control. Large groups of people, who are already socialized to look to government for their support, become complacent, expecting things from others instead of using their intelligence and imagination to create it for themselves. This creates a culture that breeds crime, addiction and other social ills.

In the 1960's, a new social class was created in America. These were individuals who said and thought that they were driven by social justice and they saw that justice as something that came from the government in the form of programs.[2] Yep! I'm talking about my generation: Woodstock, Kickapoo Creek, Sedalia, Rock festivals, drugs, and free love.....until it started to kill you. We are Baby Boomers. We are the "Me" generation. We were the paramount organizers and political activists: William Ayers, Saul Alinski, Timothy Leary. Some of us never grew up. We are still living in the 1960's and 1970's. Yes, we were rebels. The ideals of peace and love worked for us. We hated the establishment. Actually, I just wanted to party, meet chicks and play in a rock band. I could have cared less about the political climate. I was more of a hippie than a yippie.

Yes, I say unto you, we were a confused generation. Today in 2010, the very people who hated the Establishment are the Establishment. They have become everything they said they hated. Communes were in. We moved left. We turned out sociology majors by the thousands. Remember Big Brother[3]? They hated Big Brother (authoritarian control and loss of civil liberties) or at least they said they did. Now some of these folks are Big Brother. How ironic. During the time period between then and now, some perverted the entrepreneurial spirit. In the name of freedom for all, they reached out the long arm of government to create a passive, paternally marginalized citizenry.

The Millennium Generation is the generation of our parents. For the most part, they taught us morality. They were a very moral bunch. They understood integrity, honesty, and a handshake, but we challenged their ideas of right and wrong, turning the world gray for some. I am not sure why moral perceptions changed so dramatically, maybe it had to do with Viet Nam, but it has not turned out too well. The problem is; it will get worse unless someone catches on. That is why the Gen Y kids can save us, if they have a thorough understanding of their relationship to their democratic and capitalistic government. Without a doubt, they will revolt when they get the tax bill for the garbage we are now handing them. There are 80 million of them and 79 million Boomers[4]. Don't count out the Gen Xers either. They could go either way. Look out! Gen Xers are a mess right now, but they will have a rude awakening very quickly[5].

These are our kids and grandkids. What are we thinking by digging them deeper and deeper into a no-win paradigm of government spending?

Social justice reform has been around in America since the beginning of the industrial revolution. As more and more orphans, mentally ill and physically broken people were filed away in decrepit buildings and exploitive situations, church members gathered together to lobby government for regulations. At the turn of the century, basic safety nets were established to help those who could not help themselves.[6] These people who came together to help others were not advocating that government then begin to support able-bodied individuals who did not work and did not seek work training. That was the farthest thing from their intention, which was purely humanitarian for the innocent and the ill. Conversely, today's' church leaders have a tendency to abdicate their responsibilities to help the American needy to the government, while they head to Guatemala to help the poor there. Then there are the church leaders that hate America to the point that they unwittingly join the Noisemakers to achieve a justice that even they can't define. Ask the Reverend Wright in Chicago[7] what he wants America to do. I would love to hear his response.

Today's class of social justice workers sprang from the American Civil Rights Movement that demanded equality for all races. This being a noble cause, it clouded over the subsequent misuses of government powers, calling the use of tax money to support people who showed no willingness to work "social justice."

Frankly, how and why to use government funds to help others is a difficult question to ask and to answer. It requires a nation of citizens trained in analysis and understanding of their place in a capitalistic system: something we do not have. What is the difference between supporting a teenage mother with a check as she gives birth to babies and providing them with daycare through our churches and charities for children of poor men and women who are in school or working? One is taking money out with no hope of returning it and the other is support-ing the creation of money through the parents' jobs and through the education of the children. The latter encourages our natural instinct to help without coercion. Poverty in America today is not dramatic. In fact, it resembles a middle-class lifestyle in many European countries. What is dramatic are the enclosed societies of poor that circulate myths of despair, hopelessness and victimization. It is the heart-breaking failure of strong, brilliant individuals to take advantage of the opportunities around them in a more positive way. They are entrepreneurs, but their entrepreneurial spirit is perverted by a government-imposed system that violates the rules of human nature. This microcosm in the poorer sections is mimicked by the wealthy. This is natural. The bankers, Fannie Mae and Freddie Mac do exactly the same thing. When given improper and unnatural direction from Congress through regulation, they go where the entrepreneurial mind goes. They say, "Well if Congress wants us to do something stupid by loaning money to people who can't afford it, I guess we'll do it even though it is immoral. It's the law, it must be OK."

They say, "Congress can't afford what it does anyway, so why is that any different from what I am doing?" The laws of capitalistic incentive have now been violated and the system is perverted. Morals are out the door and a new morality that violates the laws of natural competition comes into being. Confused? You are supposed to be. Noisemakers create confusion and chaos for the purpose of control.

One thing that makes social justice cloudy is racism or a basic lack of human compassion. An entire race of people has been deeply traumatized. For generations they were treated with barbarity and contempt. The failure of American citizens to communicate and work together is fed in part by two poisonous rivers: racism and victimization. It is the River Hate and the River Fear.

Rather than support African Americans, Latinos and other groups with the idea that they are capable of brilliant, creative entrepreneurship, Noisemakers harp on the racists' diatribe and send out the message that there is a right-wing conspiracy to keep them down and they are victims rather than citizen actors. This, too, is a double-edged language of self hate and racism. Again, the Noisemakers are creating negative entrepreneurial endeavors; gangs, drugs, and prostitution.

These folks have generationally developed their business model. The evolution of negativity grows more negative, just as positive becomes more positive. Look at the Mexican drug wars and compare that to the progressive economic growth that America experienced the first 150 to 200 years. The fun times and criminal normalization of crime in the 1920's were followed by bad times of the Depression and The New Deal. If The New Deal had been left unchecked by WWII, it would have ruined us. (Read *New Deal Or Raw Deal* by Burton W. Folsom.) The 1950's brought growth and positive moral attitudes.[8] Since then, we have had good times and bad, but there has been a slow decline in moral values: crime, abuse, addiction and delinquency. This decline coincides with the increasing government intervention.[9]

I believe that for Americans to get back on a track of growth and strong moral values, we must work at communicating with one another.

I mean actually listening and responding, not just flinging barbs back and forth across the ever-widening chasm between right and left.

Before communication can happen between the reasonable and compassionate people of this country, they have to decide to trust one another. It's easy to say that the people of New Orleans are lazy and ought to have made something more of themselves, for example. It's racist to say that they deserved what they got when the storm hit because of their own laziness. The truth is that citizenship and optimism are not taught in public schools. Those traumatized by generations of brutality and contempt are also manipulated by corrupt political systems stemming from racism. That is the truth. The appropriate response by whites to the suffering of poor blacks in New Orleans after Katrina is, "How can I best contribute to creating a sense of self-sufficiency and citizenship for those who do not have it?"

There are some people so traumatized by the civil rights abuses in this country that they will forever identify the Democratic party or liberalism with the freedom to vote, stay in hotels and generally be treated with equality by whites. It is true that during the 1960's, highly visible people who fought for racial justice were a part of the Democratic Party. However, it is also true that George Wallace was a Democrat and Robert Byrd (Democrat) was a grand dragon in the Ku Klux Klan. It is also true that highly visible people who fought against integration and the voting rights act were members of the Republican Party. It is also true that the guy who sent troops to escort a young black girl to a white school was a Republican President named Dwight

Eisenhower. A Republican, Charlton Heston marched with Martin Luther King. It's easy to fall back on stereotypes, and I think we can all see where that's gotten us so far.

Some day we are all going to have to focus on what the sides are saying today and not what someone is telling us they are saying or what they did in the past. Political parties change according to their leadership and philosophies, while the laws of good capitalistic practice do not. We need to think it through using the positive laws of human invention and incentive.

We also want to take back our strong moral grounding that we have lost. The Ten Commandments are not an accident. Without a higher moral authority, we are left to each individual's thoughts, opinions, and illogical ideas. We can each be our own God. The Noisemakers promote this idea. Without a higher deity, they can then make themselves the religion of the day. A non-belief in God is illogical. One only need to ask themselves a few simple questions. Where and why did the Big Bang originate? How did the first cell live and why? How can nature be so perfect? This is not a question for government to decide for us. It is not for government to take our beliefs out of the public square either. We must take the time to search our own hearts and establish our place in the order of our society. As we do this individually, we become a multitude and then we act as citizens according to our values.

The tables have turned, just as they did in the time of Lincoln. Today, the conservative party is saying (most of the time), "I believe in you. I believe that you can achieve and I will not enable you in inertia, self-destruction or fear." Some day we are all going to have to stop hearing, "I want to keep you down," no matter what a Republican is saying. Yes, I admit that there are a lot of obnoxious, rich, out-of-touch and spoiled people in both parties. What we need to keep our eye on is the prize.

The prize is self-sufficiency, self-respect and solvency for each individual. As we embrace this goal, we can let go of the ravages that we faced in the days of Bobby, Martin and John, Dwight, Ronald and Charlton.

It makes no sense to think that the rich want to keep everyone poor so they can be rich. I want everyone to be rich. There is no down side to it for anyone except the Noisemakers. Rich people will have more customers and poor people can still become rich. The irony is that if the Noisemakers win, we all just get poorer, even them! As long as the Noisemakers are in control, they will have more than we do. These people are the enemy of us all.

The Noisemakers tell us "The rich get richer and the poor get poorer." This defies the natural law. When the rich get richer, the poor get richer.[10] When the poor get richer, the rich get richer, but it must happen under a capitalist entrepreneurial system. It cannot happen under centralized government control. It never has and never will. Noisemakers, through their arrogance, think that their unnatural ideas will work.

Today the Noisemakers have distorted the basic laws of a capitalistic system. They are saying they are liberals. They are not. They are Noisemakers. There are three players in this game today: conservatives, liberals and Noisemakers. The goal of the Noisemakers is to keep us from thinking it all through by keeping us from communicating reasonably and openly with one another. They divide by nature. They distort both sides.

The specter that threatens to tear us apart today is that of a seemingly well-meaning, pleasing African-American President who has been taught that government can solve the problems of the poor and disadvantaged. He is the disciple of Saul Alinsky.[11] The only thing central government can really do is offer effective, when-you-need-it education regarding capitalism and entrepreneurship. It can provide for our national defense and build a few roads and airports. The Constitution gives limited powers to the central government. The role it has incrementally accrued for itself is hurting us. We must re-think our old entrenched loyalties if we are Democrats. If we are Republicans, we better quit complaining and slinging mud and start asking, "How can I more effectively communicate and stick to my values?" We need to start talking to the regular man and woman and explain our history, our government, our Constitution and our financial system and why it is superior to others. How do I talk to folks so they don't feel threatened and demeaned?

Many conservatives have made a pretty good living just ridiculing their liberal fellow Americans. This is not an effective mind-changing method. The result is greater division. Well-meaning conservatives and liberals have become an effective tool for the Noisemakers. Conservatives use Ronald Reagan as a role model but forget he had a "big tent." Liberals may think and process differently, but they don't have a "mental disorder." If you say you want to defeat them, their emotion (fear) makes you the enemy and all logic is out the door. If they can process in a non-threatening environment and they believe you really care, they consider a helping strategy. They need to be loved or they tune out, get mad and lock up. We are all sensitive to scorn and misread intentions when threatened. If you are a Republican and you want to communicate with a Democrat, then avoid being insulting. Otherwise, you become a bad person in their eyes and all communication ceases. As in any speech where love is absent you are no more than a clanging gong and sounding cymbal.

High personal emotions are close to the surface on both sides and the Noisemakers exploit this.

We can commit to capitalism and economic solvency all day long but if we do not love one another, we will still fail as a nation.

There is no blanket answer. There is no government program that can be left to grow and morph from year to year. Every single penny that the United States government spends should be balanced by five to ten pennies that its citizens earn and create through entrepreneurship. If that is not happening, we as Americans must make it happen. The question is why aren't we doing just that? The answer is that we're fighting with each other. We're calling each other names: "dirty liberal", "greedy conservative," "corporate rapist," "socialist," "fat cat banker" etc.

The truth is that we're all inventors at heart. Some of us invent ways to deal with human systems and some of us invent products and services. The key is for us to work together with the common goal of sustaining a solvent, growing economy and a fair society.

Here are some examples of welfare that most people don't realize are "welfare."

1. Cash for clunkers

2. Incentives for new home buyers

3. Pell grants

4. Farm subsidies

5. Earned income tax credit

6. Cap and trade

The list goes on and on and on. There are thousands of ways that government subsidizes the populations. These are essentially a bribe for a vote and a dilution of a capitalist economy.

Noisemakers want you to believe that right-wingers are anti-gay people. If you listen to what they say, conservatives and Republicans are always racist and homophobes. They are self-satisfied, greedy individuals who think the hardworking poor are just not working hard enough. The Noisemakers paint all Republicans as people who would rather pollute for their short-term gain than preserve the environment for future generations.

Two things are non-negotiable: 1) You have to earn at least what you spend, ideally more and, 2) You cannot ignore the environment without harming yourself and others. Both conservatives and liberals know this, but the Noisemakers convince one side that the other does not.

Since this book is about economics and investing, I will stick to talking about economic imperatives and leave the environmental imperatives to someone else. Keep in mind that the Noisemakers are using the environmental issues to divide us and to bring us down to economic equality with the rest of the world. It is easier to control if everyone is in the same boat. If one country is out-performing the rest of the world, it is impossible to get the citizens of that country to be more like the others and welcome their lowered level of lifestyle comfort. The ideas of cap and trade and the EPA come from those concerned about global warming. While their goals may be worthy, they have not carefully considered the way that a people accustomed to capitalistic enterprise will respond to a lowering of the lifestyle they worked hard to create. Instead of trying to force the current cap and trade controls on a capitalistic populace, global warming policy makers need to go back to the drawing board. I have a healthy skepticism about global warming when the very same people in the 1970's told us we were heading into an ice age. I see they have changed the term "global warming" to "climate change." I guess they don't want to get caught again with their pants down so they have covered all bases. Think about it.

This environmental quagmire and the healthcare system can give Noisemakers a great deal of central government control over our lives…if we let them. Remember, we are our government. Those who lead you to believe that there is a magic circle surrounding the United States of America that makes everything all right when we designate government funds to provide goods and services are lying to you. Those repudiating this trend and saying that people must work and earn the money to pay for those same goods and services are telling you the truth.

As I write this book in 2010, many Americans are facing joblessness[13]. The reason they are facing that joblessness is because they failed to understand these issues, were not taught their relationship to a capitalist system and did not hold their government accountable.

In the current environment where Democrats are rushing to hurt while calling it "help" and Republicans are screaming and yelling in anger and frustration, celebrities like Rush Limbaugh are quickly pegged as inflammatory loudmouths. Rush does have an intentionally provocative personality, but that does not mean that he is bad or wrong. In fact, if you listen to him, he is pointing out who the real Noisemakers are. Today's Noisemakers are the Obamas, the Clintons, the Alinski's, Al Gore and those who stump for government programs, government solutions and government money to alleviate the economic, environmental and social woes of America. I could include Nancy Pelosi and Harry Reid and other big government senators and congressmen, but they are mostly useful mouthpieces.

The two sides, right and left, don't have moral equivalency. The right, for whatever reason, wears the historical badge of racism and classism, but it is actually talking today – at the present moment – about basic self-respect and self-discipline and an ordered way of living that allows each individual to earn enough to support themselves.

The left wears the historical badge of social justice, but it is talking today about paternalism, colonization via subsidized housing and rubber-stamping mediocrity in the name of "making it right."

The reason we are so gullible today, believing in the magic of government spending and programs, is that we have been fed propaganda for over three generations. It takes three generations to trap people in a system where you feed people the information that you are "helping" them when you are really systematically disempowering them and enlarging government.

When someone points this reality out, the Noisemakers call him or her a racist. In a speech in Missouri during his campaign, President

Obama said, "We are going to fundamentally change the country."[14] He made a speech about how bad the fat cat bankers are. It is the free rein that government gave bankers to manipulate the market that needs to be changed. I ask you, why would we want to fundamentally change America? You cannot change the nation's fundamentals unless you change it into a non-capitalistic, non-democratic society and throw away our Constitution by calling it a "living, breathing document."

The 1960's were a groundbreaking time in our history. Many Americans would like to stay in that "rainbow" moment. We want Obama to be another King or Kennedy. Fantasy can be very expensive at this point.

News to liberals: Being a conservative does not mean you want to defeat and hold back black people. I think the origin of this belief comes from the fact that slavery made money. Slavery was embraced by many people as a fiscal solution, an entrepreneurial idea. Now is the time to step out of the trauma of slavery and the trauma of racism long enough to see that today's Republicans and fiscal conservatives are not slaveowners, nor would they ever support a fiscal approach that dehumanized and harmed others. Let's realize that post-traumatic reactive mode doesn't help us. You know what hurt black people just as much as slavery? Paternalism[15] did and does. Paternalism is treating someone as if they are a child and cannot do things for themselves; acting as a parent who "knows better."

Naturally, a person cannot receive free stuff without wanting more free stuff. Who wouldn't? Paternalism is paternalism. It started out on the slave block and now it's disguised as a host of compassionate liberal government programs. Nothing works unless you work for it. News for conservatives: Being a liberal does not mean you want to hand people a check. It means you want to help them improve, grow and be successful Americans.

The truth is that this country is our business. We have to run our own affairs and our own political actions just like we were balancing the books. We have to look at ourselves and say, "I create everything that happens to me." All of the money that the government spends is my money and your money. One way or another we will pay for it. When faced with challenges, we all have to say to ourselves, "My only real solution is to be inventive, imaginative and optimistic. I have to believe in myself and make opportunities where none exist. I have to see capitalism for what it is: a canvas, a pliable reality that I can mold if I will with my own energy."

The majority of the American people are reasonable. They are neither narcissistic, greedy racists nor lazy, lying socialists. By the way, Noisemakers are not socialists or communists; they don't care about owning our companies and industries, because they are perfectly satisfied with controlling them via regulations and taxes. (For our own good, of course.) However, natural negative progression dictates that they will control our companies someday. Noisemakers are incrementalists.

As time progressed through the 1960's on, the public schools
in the United States abandoned the teaching of the free enterprise
capitalistic system. I read my fourth grade daughter's economic textbook 15 or so years ago and it had a whole chapter about communism
and one brief paragraph on capitalism that basically said, "Capitalism is
a system in which the government cannot tell companies what to do."
End of story. Americans today don't know the relationship between the
individual's relationship to capitalism and the individual's relationship to
socialism.

When we spend all of our money and the system we've created
eats itself through the re-distribution of wealth, then we will self-
destruct. Capitalism creates from nothing and will self-destruct when
there is no innovation or incentive. The same people end up on the top
eventually, whether they are right or left because they are the people
who can practice innovation. In socialism or in despotic governments, an
elite few live on the top and keep it that way. Capitalism is the enemy of
central government control because it thrives on innovation and effi-
ciency.

My kids say I'm still a kid. One day, I heard them complaining
about how they didn't want to go on an outing with their friend's parents. I said, "You go places with me," to which they replied sarcastically,
" You are like hanging around with another kid." I like that.

Anyway, I started with somewhat less than nothing. In fact,
one time I had to go to a small grocery store and borrow a loaf of bread

and a pack of baloney until my first paycheck. The store manager even threw in a bottle of ketchup. This is my favorite sandwich even today, darn carbs though. I also loved those Swanson chicken pot pies and those little round tubs of macaroni and cheese. I could eat a meal for 17 cents for chicken and 12 cents for the mac and cheese. I ate this every day for weeks when I was broke. I tried the chicken pot pie the other day and it stunk. They took out most of the chicken! I'll never buy another. It cost a lot more than 17 cents too! I ate those pot pies because I was working at Stapleton International Airport in Denver scrubbing, stripping and waxing the floors on the concourses and watching all those rich folk getting off the airplanes. I was the only white guy (except the supervisor, of course). I learned a lot from my black co-workers. I learned how to not get caught drinking gin in the bathroom and how to score with "chicks." I taught them about white "chicks" and hippies. We had fun. What I also learned is that everyone has the same dreams and ambitions.

We all wanted to be those rich people getting off those planes. I decided then and there that I was gonna do it by starting my own businesses. I had many and varied jobs after that that gave me a very unique and diverse set of skills and abilities. Eventually, I became a business owner. Many people say they want to start a business, but they don't. They don't because they like living "risk-free" or at least as small amount of risk as possible. There is no such thing as living risk-free. They think this way because, as I said, they have not learned what the relationship of the individual is to a capitalist economy. They don't see the big picture. They don't think it through. They are actually creating more risk by not thinking entrepreneurially. You don't have to own your own business to be entrepreneurial, but you must create value for yourself and your employer. Your reward will be in direct relation to the number of people you serve. Notice I said reward, not money.

What most people don't seem to understand is that many times the business owner is the least paid person. This is especially true in a centrally controlled system. When a successful businessman or woman is made less profitable by centrally controlled regulation and taxes, they revolt and dump the business. The employees lose their jobs and new money stops being created. See the risk here? The business owner must have the opportunity to become rich under his or her own creative effort. Otherwise, why do it? This is a law of human initiative. The most disgraceful thing going on today is that most Noisemakers have never made a payroll with their own money, but they are telling us what we need to do. They live in the theoretical world of academia.

Bill Gates went out and started a company in a garage. When he did that, he created new money in a capitalistic system. He didn't print money; he created money where none existed. It started the greatest economic boom in human history. He sought out and found investors who had money and wanted to voluntarily put their money into his idea. This enabled Bill Gates to expand his business, make more money and create jobs. In fact, if you owned Microsoft stock in your 401k, you undoubtedly made money. You could have gotten rich and never stepped foot in a Microsoft building just by owning his stock. The government can never do this. Governments do not create profit, only expense. The more Microsoft is taxed, the less they make, the less you make, the fewer jobs are created and the worse the economy does. It's the natural law.

If you worked at Microsoft, you got shares, plus a 401k and a paying job. At the end of your employment there, you could sell the stock you owned. No matter where you come from in society, you can save. In a capitalistic society, when the rich get richer, the poor get richer.

When the populace is tricked into believing that they can rely on the government to "bail them out" then they are putting the nails in the casket, so-to-speak. Whatever is created in a government rescue is created by the government and that money has to come out of the pockets of the people. P.S. You! It's a process of shuffling funds from person-to-person and even from people who work to people who don't work. This is the Noisemakers' goal. This situation makes it more difficult to create jobs because the investment level isn't there. It creates an economic death spiral.

You can look at different states today and see the spiral. We as Americans are falling off the ends of the earth economically because of excessive government spending and taxing. Massive numbers of people are moving to states like Texas that have no state income tax and a budget surplus. This is as it should be. Competition amongst states was envisioned by our founders. They knew it would create prosperity and keep state governments honest and productive. If we didn't like the policies of one state, we could at least get away. They were fearful of a strong central government and wrote the Constitution to reflect such. We now have an overwhelming federal government that is ruling over us and our states. The federal response from the Noisemakers will be to cripple the higher performing states by regulation, probably from an environmental and health care stance.

Government by its nature spends more rather than less. Bureaucrats create more bureaucracies. That's how they advance their own careers. They enlarge and are continually in charge of more people by creating more regulation. It will never stop on its own and must be controlled by you. You do this by electing people who pledge to keep the government under control and small. By the way, this is mandated by our Constitution.[16] The Noisemakers' goal is exactly the opposite. They want control and to get it they have to weaken the safeguards we have in place. They say they are curtailing spending when they are not. One of their tricks is baseline budgeting. If eight percent is the baseline, then an increase of eight percent is a zero percent increase. When you base a whole society on these faulty concepts and getting votes to support these concepts, then the logical outcome is that the system collapses.

Friends, the Noisemakers don't mind if the system collapses. They will just glibly convince us that they will fix it. They thrive on crisis, real or perceived. If there isn't one, they'll create one knowingly or by implementing their crazy programs. They will tell us we just need to give them more control. They say that the failed policies of the past will not work, but they are referring to basic hands off capitalism, not over-regulation.

They will say what we are willing to hear, "Greedy (out-of-control) capitalists are the problem." We will swallow anything they say if we think it will help and more than likely, most of us won't have a clue what they are saying. I'll guarantee you one thing: it will sound fabulous! I will guarantee another thing: It won't work. Right now ask yourself how much you really know about how capital is formed and how our system works. I can tell you from my experience in teaching adults about our system for the last 20-odd years, you don't know what you don't know and I don't care if you are rich or poor. Americans don't understand capitalism.

No matter what side you live on right now, our financial system is broken and it won't work. Government is a system of gates that are controlled by individuals who are susceptible to corruption for personal gain. Certainly, if we lived in a utopia and distributed money to those who needed it and taught them how to make money for themselves within a short period, then the money they received would pay for itself. Unfortunately, what we have is an indiscriminate system being skimmed by citizens and government officials alike.

The hard-working individual in the middle loses out and loses faith in the capitalist system. I personally don't know if the existing situation is a purposeful assault or a natural progression. I think it is probably a little of both, but it doesn't matter, it is messed up. I do know that it has accelerated in the last nine years, from 2000 to 2008 during the George W. Bush Administration. The Democrats had control of Congress and the Bush family has a bad habit of giving in to political pressure. Now that the Noisemakers are in complete control, we are traveling down the road of financial doom at the speed of light. It has been a perfect storm for Noisemakers. The newly elected administration promised to be our saviors when in reality it has become obvious they are our destructors.

The Noisemakers were prepared for this. They have been rehearsing, planning and incrementally implementing central control for years. They are now almost totally unchecked. They have abandoned any pretense and have become unbelievably blatant in their disdain for liberals and conservatives. They have increased the noise and driven the divisiveness to never-before-seen heights. It is a feeding frenzy of wolves or lions over a kill. We are the prey, they are the carnivores. They have shot us dead and are taking our head to the taxidermist to hang on their wall. We are being shot and stuffed.

The general public harbors a misconception that government has money. They have only what they confiscate from us in the form of taxes. We as individual citizens pay for everything. We pay for all corporate taxes, all lawsuits, all health costs and every one of the government agencies and employees; most people are living paycheck to paycheck. Because we don't teach in schools the relationship of the individual to the capitalist economy, adults, as they enter the work force don't understand how they can best provide for themselves.

In an educated society, where people understand how their capitalistic economy works, they would not fail to save, use credit beyond their means or vote for politicians who tax and spend. Even the wealthy don't understand how the system works; they have sunk down into their own sense of comfort and entitlement and fail to examine the mechanisms that put them where they are today.

Government cannot teach people not to abuse power and money. Government cannot teach people to act with equity and discipline. Either we will learn how to do these things because we realize that if we don't we will die, or we will die. There is a real question today as to whether or not the United States of America will survive. If we do survive, it will be because each person decides to change his or her thinking not because of anything that the government does. It's easy to point fingers at the greedy opportunists, as the Noisemakers are doing, but we have learned that what is easy is usually wrong.

For example, Obama came on TV and said that the "bad" bankers had walked away with 10M, but really, those bankers walked away with 10M in stock options.[17] Stock options are not cash; they are a promise to pay if the company performs well. This is Obama being a Noisemaker. The Noisemakers feed off of our ignorance and excess. They are parasites and when we crumble, they will too.

Make no mistake. I am a radical and I am writing this book to ask you to be a radical too. A radical changes things. Each person needs to make a decision to change the way they think, listen and act. We must think about things instead of reacting to who said it.

The government-controlled public educational system trained us not to question. They gave us linear thinking. Because Americans are more comfortable, even in poverty, than most people in the world, we don't pay attention. We make the mistake of trusting government and we don't participate in anything more than a kind of herd action once in a while. Today's Tea Party Movement is an exception. These are Americans who are participating just as our forefathers anticipated we would. Who knows? They may just save this country.

It is the nature of government to encroach upon the liberties of the people and it is the job of every citizen to watch and warn their government when it has crossed important boundaries. We have relinquished that job for watching TV, going out to eat and letting other people tell us how to think. All the while, government operates a divide-and-conquer strategy, fragmenting people into segments, planting Noisemakers to confuse us and pitting us against one another.

Government is basically a film of Vaseline over the windshield of capitalism. You think you might be going toward affluence and safety, but who knows? The less government on the windshield the better. The caveat to that statement is that we must take responsibility as citizens for how we think about money, government, race and success. If you want less government, look at yourself and develop more self-discipline. The average American does not think through their spending and saving choices. If they do, they still allow themselves to participate in hateful, angry demonization of others.

In 1973 Carter said every American has the right to own a house and he created the Fair Housing Act [18] When he did this, he said to banks, "Go ahead and lend to people who are bad credit risks. If they default, the government will pick up the tab. The government may insure mortgages or just bail people and institutions out at the cost of the taxpayer." Carter in his false "social justice" role really sent the message to lower-income Americans, "I don't believe you can make it like everybody else."

In his administration, Bill Clinton started funding the Fair Housing Act. Or should I be more accurate and say that his Congress did.[19] Greenspan kept interest rates low to encourage the economy and stimulate buying of things. The ones who could least afford it were encouraged to borrow to buy the American dream (their own home) and credit flowed freely. Everyone who offered these mortgages made money; investment companies bought them, realized that they would default and insured them by selling off derivatives. Every time they sold, they made a fee and commission for selling. The entire spiral into a national financial depression started with an erroneous value system that was codified into government regulation and then exploited by greedy opportunists.

The average American says, "I believe the work I do is way too valuable for me to be making this small amount of money." They look at wealthy people and ask, "Why should these people have this much money when I only have this much money?" Because they have not been taught how to think about government and economics and their place within the system, they decide, naturally, that there is a lack of fairness that needs to be addressed. In fact, the lack of fairness goes the other way, those who are not working or are not endeavoring to work should have even less money than they have. In a capitalist system, the richer individuals become, the more money they create for those whom they employ and train.

Teachers are a good example of the kind of skewed thinking about earning power that I just described. Success is defined as the progressive realization of worthy ideas, not as money. You know when you become a teacher that it doesn't pay well. To make a lot of money as a teacher, you would have to start your own school.

You can't start your own school without massive capital because government regulates the schools so they cannot compete. Education is the biggest monopoly in the world. Public and private schools turn out clones and knowledge comes from what they can read from other people's writings. Most students don't think beyond their comfort zone and the structure the school allows. Don't get me wrong, we have some great teachers, but they are only allowed to follow directions laid out by various beauracracies.

Unions are another example of malfunctioning government. Initially designed to protect the worker against exploitive employers, unions now exploit the worker for the sake of the organization, i.e., the power and wealth of a few. Nurses don't realize that in a government system they will be unionized and their only opportunity for advancement will come from seniority and they will have no incentive or a path for advancement because of superior ability or hard work. The patient becomes a liability for both the nurse and limited government resources. In the government system the patient is a liability not an asset. What I mean is, when people stop functioning as individuals who earn and relinquish their decision-making power to a group representative, and then they stop earning and start costing. If you ran a candy store and you ate candy for breakfast, lunch and dinner you would not make money and you would get sick. When you work for a living and then you start charging yourself via taxes and union fees for the right to work and earn money, you are not making any money and you are going to collapse financially.

Yes, there are people who go out and spend, purchase and live paycheck to paycheck. The savings rate went down to a negligible number in the last 10 years. We have seen in the United States a massive use of credit, why is this?[20] Dangerous credit extension has been created by the government's interference in banks and mortgage lending rates. Again, we as citizens have been duped into believing that the easy credit came from someone or something else. In fact, easy credit came from a collusion between government policy and the willingness of banks to make a profit. As citizens, we did our perceived but deadly part, we borrowed. Now, the easy credit has disappeared and we are the ones who are responsible. We are responsible for not holding our government accountable, for not paying attention and for swallowing whatever we are fed in school. It may be comfortable not to question or to push the open purse closed, but it isn't really a choice. We either do it now, or we face the consequences later.

As any coach will tell you, if you want to win, you have to win within yourself first. For example, long ago, teachers taught students how to think. They explained that if you plan to borrow 25k, you need to ask yourself, "What would that mean to me as an individual? What will happen if I get to a point where I cannot pay it back?" The unspoken wisdom today is that an individual can always declare bankruptcy. Where is the teacher who teaches the student that they will pay double and triple for that bankruptcy in the end? It may be embedded in the $200k price tag their kid faces if he or she wants to go to college. It may be in the groceries they buy or their health insurance costs or their taxes.

Instead, today's consumer lives in a teenage mentality of envy. He or she looks at Larry's car and asks themselves, "How does Larry have this car and I don't? What is the difference between me and Larry? I am just as good as he is. I work harder. I want to have a car like Larry's" or "I don't want Larry to have such a nice car when I can't have one too." Either way, where is the understanding of his or her relationship to the capitalist system? Where is the willingness to investigate and innovate within that system?

Just when money becomes too tight because of excessive use of credit, a guy comes along and says, "I'm going to fix it for you. We'll make your mortgage go away if you vote for us."

When asked how she viewed the current Obama administration, one woman who voted for him said (and I am paraphrasing) something like, "I haven't gotten my check yet: my Obama check, from his stash. He bailed out the banks he can get money out of his stash for me."

This begs the question, how did government in previous administrations manage to mismanage the banking system to such an extent? In an oblique way, Obama is addressing government excesses by several previous administrations towards banks and mortgage lenders. The problem is: 1) the average American does not understand what caused the problem, and they are perfectly willing to use the same government involvement to fix it, which obviously won't work. 2) Obama is directing his energies toward creating more government rather than teaching and empowering the individual to radically alter their approach to citizenship and financial stewardship. He stood on a platform of hope and change but the truth is he's no more of a radical than the rest of Americans. We need a leader who will cut the crap and refuse to keep the political peace at the expense of the people.

As I said earlier, the number of people taking money out of the government in order to survive is rapidly approaching the number of people putting money into the system. When are we as a people going to wake up, kick out the Noisemakers, talk to one another and seize our economy before it goes down the deep pockets of corrupt systems, whether they are in business or in government welfare?

Everything that happens in this world inside of us and outside of us begins with a thought. How we think determines how we live. Before solvency comes analysis and contemplation. As a people, as individuals, we must think things through over and over again. We must learn to check and recheck our actions. We must understand the big picture and realize that it is us. Things don't "happen." We create them through our thoughts and then the actions or lack of actions that stem from those thoughts.

What do you think will happen if you tax rich people more? Put yourself in their spot in a realistic way and think it through. If your answer is, "They won't be able to save as much," then keep thinking.

In fact, the answer is that they won't be able to create jobs. This may eliminate YOUR job. People in the USSR understand this now but they didn't know what to do when they went under. They are more than 200 years behind us. We know what to do, but we are not doing it. We do not understand that we can actually go under. They are trying to become us and we are (unwittingly) trying to become them. Hmm, which sounds better to you?

I have a friend that just told me that Bush couldn't destroy the economy and neither can Obama. Bush had a deficient his last year of 500 billion. (Like how much you would spend over and above your paycheck every year) Obama's this year is 1.5 trillion. (1 trillion=1000 billion.) Congress just raised the debt ceiling to over 12 trillion. Our country's gross domestic product (like your gross paycheck) is 14 trillion. They are going to add to this debt every year just as we have in the past. How long could you do this at your house and survive? This ain't rocket science.

The Noisemakers are winning.

Are the Noisemakers winning?

You decide.

Noise Level Check: Chapter 1

Finish these sentences:

1. When I am working in a business and I find a process that is not working well I think:

   a. Whoever created this is stupid.

   b. How can I create a better process and sell it to management?

   c. Every company has some waste, it's not so bad.

   d. I'll pick my battles and live with this.

   e. I can run a company that is leaner and lighter than this one.

   f. It's a job and I need the money. Other people get paid to deal with this kind of thing.

   Look at the choice you made. After two years, what will be the natural outcome of your choice of thoughts?

2. When I hear about government budgeting and spending I think:

   a. Boring.

   b. As long as they don't raise taxes, I don't really care.

c. Those people don't have a clue what it's like for regular folks like me.

d. I'm going to call and write my representatives about this.

e. I wonder what my friends and neighbors think about these spending justifications.

f. I'm going to research that bill and write about it on my blog.

3. Where will your choice from the list of thoughts above lead in one year?

4. What will be the effect of your choice of thoughts on your friends and family?

5. How will your choice of thought affect your life?

Do you have additional thoughts you would like to share with me about this chapter, or questions? I want to know what you think! Email me at steve@thenoisemakersbook.com.

But what do we mean by the American Revolution?

Do we mean the American war?

The Revolution was effected before the war commenced.

The Revolution was in the minds and hearts of the people;

a change in their religious sentiments, of their duties and

obligations...This radical change in the principles,

opinions, sentiments, and affections of the people

was the real American Revolution.

~ John Adams, letter to H. Niles,

February 13, 1818

Where Did Our Money Go?

and

Who Shot Us In The Fannie Mae?

Who made a profit while we were hung out to dry?

I'm not going to get distracted by giving an in-depth analysis of the collapse of the credit markets, but it deserves a little time to explain why the unnatural manipulations of market forces by government and regulatory bodies always turn out poorly and always will. As I said earlier, the debacle actually started in the Carter years when the Democrats decided it would be a good idea for everyone to own the American dream — their own home. Not much happened, though. Carter ran out of money and Reagan never wanted to do much with it and the democratic congress knew he would never sign a bill to fund it anyway. Then along came Bill Clinton and he decided to fund the proposition because, well that's what Democrats do: fund. They accused banks of red lining (not giving loans in minority neighborhoods) and pressured banks using surrogates like Jesse Jackson[1]. They used their influence to pressure financial institutions to give loans to folks who had no means to pay the loans back. I guess they thought the government could come in and be the savior when folks started to lose their homes. This is a Noisemaker strategy.

It became a money-making boom. Everyone was making money. Well, you know the outcome. You lost. Many of those in political power won. Franklin Raines and Jamie Garelick, administrators of Fannie Mae, got tens of millions of dollars (100 million for Raines and 75 million for Garelick)[2] even while the Office of Mangement and Budget found massive fraud and that bonuses were given using false numbers.[3] Congress ignored the fraud and the findings and congressmen and women from both parties walked away with a total of 354 million dollars in campaign contributions. What do you think would have happened if Garelick and Raines had either been Republicans or corporate CEOs?

Jesse Jackson and Acorn got a large sum.[4] Obama and Dodd were the two largest congressional recipients, then Schumer and Frank. In 2005, McCain tried to pass the Federal Housing Enterprise Regulatory Reform Act, but it was blocked by the Democrats with all of the big four recipients voting "No."

Raines and Garelick were fined about 30% of what they actually made. You may know the rest of the story. You lost your ass (financially speaking), while government officials and corporate heads kept the dough. They kept the dough even while they were being bailed out by you-know-who. This was an involuntary investment by you with no hope of you ever getting any of it back. Most of the TARP has been paid back with interest. I just don't think you got a check for your account yet, huh? This is a long and depressing story, but I'm gonna concentrate on you.

When Noisemakers start manipulating, you will always lose. It may even appear that you are winning, but in the long run YOU lose. When they attack rich folk, YOU lose. When they attack big oil, YOU lose. When they attack big health insurance, doctors and corporations, YOU lose. Any attack on any positive enterprise will always have the effect of YOU losing. Remember when the Noisemakers were demonizing the big oil companies for excess and exorbitant profits? The only thing in your 401k that was making money during that time was the oil and energy investments. So what was the result of the demonization? Your 401k went down and hundreds of thousands of jobs were lost.

You say, "But Steve, we were paying astronomical prices at the pumps for gas." I always advise my clients to own what they hate to buy. If you owned the gas or oil you were happy, right? Not just the stock, but the actual oil and gas or invested in the drilling for oil and gas. Why didn't you? Probably because you didn't know how. You mean your broker didn't recommend it? No he didn't. Why not! He or she doesn't sell it. Probably doesn't even know how it works and it is not in their port-folio either. The typical stockbroker sells two products: stocks and bonds. I am going to teach you about the others. Why? So you don't have to risk your entire portfolio in only stocks and bonds, and when gas prices go up, you will just say YES,YES, YES.

There are eight or nine asset classes, and most investors have two. Sound ridiculous? It is! Before this is over, you will at least know about the other classes of assets in which you can invest if you choose. It doesn't mean you have to use them, but your life will never be the same after you finish this book. There are forces in play that hurt all in-vesting, so for you to use the system to your advantage, we have to un-derstand more than just what the asset classes are; we have to preserve the free enterprise system in a positive way so that we may ALL pros-per. The Noisemakers are not going to like you having this information. An educated citizenry steals their power.

The scary thing is that the Noisemakers are extremely organized. Today, the Noisemakers have hidden themselves in the extreme left wing of the Democratic Party. They are not really Democrats, as I said ear-lier, they are a third group, "Noisemakers" disguised as Democrats.

They have stolen valid ideas and perverted them to fit the model of oppression while at the same time declaring they are just here to help us. Can Noisemakers ever be disguised as the right wing? Of course they can! Right or left, they would be the same people. They would only change their speech. Noisemakers merely identify with the party they're in, and try and change the natural positive laws of capitalistic growth. It just so happens that Noisemakers are manipulating us from their hiding place on the left today. They have found it easier in today's political environment to exploit the helpers and liberal thinkers.

Helpers (liberals) are more emotionally driven than Builders (conservatives). Builders are more driven by the logic and less by emotion. We need both for balance. Ideally, the Helpers would trust the Builders' logic and the Builders would trust the Helpers compassion and desire to help. For us to work together, we must trust one another and possess a common understanding. We must stand together upholding the natural motivations of the free spirit and the positive spiritual drive of man. Without this common bond, we will fall into a world of despair.

"The Ten Commandments" and *The Constitution of the United States of America* stand as spiritual and political standards for us to follow. Have you noticed that the Constitution can be distorted by man, but "The Ten Commandments" cannot? We all know which one came first and who wrote 'em. Both documents are extraordinarily simple. You cannot amend "The Ten Commandments." The framers made it extremely hard to amend the *Constitution* but left it to the interpretation of the Supreme Court. I believe *The Constitution* was divinely inspired. It is just too darn good for mankind to be able to come up with this on our own and, if you read the writings of our framers and *The Constitution* itself, you see that they believed this also. Our heritage and history repeats this theme over and over. "In God we trust," is on our money. "I swear to tell the truth so help me, God," not "So help me Me." Look at the world before the United States. It was an evil mess. People were always ruled over. There was no such thing as self-government. Look what we have done in just a couple of hundred years to become the greatest force for good and justice the world has ever seen. We are not perfect because we are human, but we keep trying and growing. Central control was to be shunned, always, end of story. The greatest fear our founders had was tyrannical control from the federal government.

We have been steadily moving in the wrong direction for decades now and it is beginning to show in our economy. We are in more wars than just the war against terrorists; we are in a fight for our very souls, our personal money, our economy and our freedom from progressive centrally controlled tyranny.

One major problem we are having today is that the Right is being suckered into the, "who can win the argument today" mentality. The Builders are angry and frustrated and they are driving the Helpers away and locking them up mentally. You cannot change a person's mind by beating them up. When you speak in anger, you just create a negative reaction. I know a lot, if not all, of this is going to be hard to swallow for some folks, but just promise me you will try to think it through. Don't react emotionally for a bit. Just think. Finish the book. Meditate and absorb. Then let me know what you think and feel. I believe that the leadership in today's Democratic Party is seeking to destroy the capitalist system as we know it in the United States and replace it with a controlled capitalist system. Noisemakers will have a controlled capitalist system for their own gain. Each day it becomes clearer. The rank and file sincerely believes that they are being good Helpers and that they are not corrupting the system more than the poverty levels do. In retrospect, however, we can see that it is not just a matter of making adjustments to the free market economy, but it is also a matter of interfering with the entrepreneurial drive of the masses. Those who circumvent and resist increasingly restrictive and useless regulations are frustrated capitalists.

If reasonable regulations were to be written, most people would comply because they wish for fair competition. Unreasonable regulations cause a natural surge of revolt, consciously and subconsciously, among the people. Regulations can also be written to intentionally alter fair competition. This is what central control has the ability to do. One technique they use today is unionization. In its most pure form, a centrally controlled government system is a union with controlled costs, incomes and outcomes for its citizens. Seniority rules in a union. The most unfair competition in the world is when the government directly controls a business as with General Motors and the banks. In a centrally controlled system which we have today, the government controls or highly influences several key areas: the education system (NEA, TEA), the media NBC,CBS,CNN,MSNBC, ABC, The Times etc.), the banks, the FED and recently the major banks such as Bank of America, Wells Fargo, Citi Bank etc.[5] The last thing to fall is YOU! How better to control you than to control your health care? Think about it. We are seeing unprecedented government control at this time in history. Of course, the Noisemakers tell us that it is for our own good and protection from the greedy fat cat bankers, health insurers and doctors. This is the road-of-no-return to central control. If America survives, it will only be a shadow of itself and will leave a void that will leave the world open to the black hearts of the world. We just won't have the money to respond. We won't have the resources to respond to natural disasters nationally and personally and we won't have the resources to donate. There can be no other result. The world will enter a time of chaos because there will be no major force for good in the world. America will lose her place. We can certainly talk about being a force for good, but we will be broke.

The weakest point of any human system is the humans themselves. A nation of people willing to sacrifice one another for short-term financial or political gains will not stand. I am writing this book because I believe that we are a nation of good people; people who can and will make choices in their own lives to be self-disciplined and people who will more actively participate in their government. Just as a reminder, the great experiment in which we are involved is called "self-government." When any one legitimate segment of our population feels ruled over, they will revolt. This is why we must understand and continually think through what people are saying and whether it can work following the progression of positive growth. Some say we must not be judgmental. On the contrary, we must root out the false prophets, in other words, the Noisemakers, so that we may continue to be the great force for good that the United States has always been.

If you look at individuals like Bernie Madoff and John Stanford, people who have violated SEC regulations and defrauded investors, you see examples of the opposite of true entrepreneurialism. These people would argue that once the government starts creating rules that make no sense, smart people will go where the money can be made regardless of ethics. For example, they figure out a way to make money from cheap credit. They do not ask, "How can we help our customer?" but "How can we find our way around the regulations so we can make money?"

True entrepreneurialism, however, is a product of forethought, self-discipline and, of course, integrity. Madoff (Stanford is still being sorted out) participated in a simple ponzi scheme where new investors' money was given to old investors to show a fabulous return and therefore attract even more money, while at the same time declaring only the unique and privileged individual may participate. This ponzi scheme occurred under the most highly regulated industry on earth. My point? No matter how many regulations are passed, the simplest fraud in the world can still work. One of the largest expenses investment companies pay today is for regulation compliance. I shouldn't say investment companies are paying, because YOU pay for it. In other words, you experience higher fees, lower returns and less affluence upon retiring.

No one in the financial investment industry seems to know just what is legal and what is not. They don't know the rule *de jour*. Interpretation changes. A well written rule is simple and easy to understand, and a poorly written one begs for abuse because it seems, and is, dumb. It conflicts with the investor's (customer's) benefit. Many times, the rule-makers have no practical experience in the business that they are regulating. They may even be the buddy of a politician and are getting some of the spoils of victory. Regulators and Noisemakers by their very nature react with more of the same. When something bad happens they always think the answer is more regulation and more oversight. This means more cost to the investor –YOU. Even sensible guys like Bill O'Reilly fall for this kind of regulation in order to "protect the folks" He knoweth not what he asketh!

Madoff's scheme was the oldest and simplest scheme that exists and they could not stop it. The regulations were in place and the regulators were reviewing his books. He was even being turned in by his competition. Rest assured, the Noisemakers have moved in to espouse the evils of the capitalist system. They want to remake the financial industry by increased rules and oversight. The natural progression of this regulation will mean that you will make less money in your 401k and other investments and there will be even more confusion in compliance departments. Therefore, there will be more interpretation violations, more fines, more regulations and more bad reputations. We will be faced with more Enrons and Madoffs and less customer trust and less money. Fewer businesses will be formed, fewer jobs created and more fines and on and on and on. The result - YOU LOSE. The Noisemakers win for a while, but because no new money is raised, they lose also and the world is exposed to despotism. A new dark age threatens to dawn for our children and grandchildren. It can happen. Don't think for a minute it can't. Today, the Noisemakers are the strongest they have ever been.

"Steve, it sounds so bleak," you may say. As many know and have practiced in the past, our recourse to the encroachment of government is civil action: voting, vocal opposition and grassroots protests such as the current Tea Party Movement. When enterprising people begin saying, "This regulation doesn't make sense" or "I don't agree with it so I will circumvent it," we're all in trouble. Not the kind of trouble we traditionally think of, however. We become involved in unnatural negative progression. Man will always revolt against the truly unjust, especially Americans! Instead of blindly obeying a ridiculous rule or regulation, we will find ways around it. The battle is no longer to produce a useful product or service, but to simply beat the rule and rule makers that are ruling over us. This is why the tax code is thousands of pages long. Confiscating money from people brings revolt, even from those who do the confiscations. Our present head of the IRS, Treasury Secretary Timothy Geithner, was caught not paying his taxes.[6] His excuse was it was an oversight. Right! Tom Daschle and Charles Rangle, to name others, have been caught in tax "indiscretions." These are the very folks advocating increased taxes. If this were a positive endeavor, one would think they would put in extra money. This is easy to understand however: Noisemakers feel superior to us and therefore exempt themselves from the rules of the masses.

So many businesses are now simply responding to regulations instead of providing for their customers. Morals become secondary as these companies fight for survival and create value for their shareholders....YOU! The Noisemakers have put corporate heads in a no-win situation. Moral business leaders naturally put the customer first and when regulations actually hurt their customers they are caught in a moral dilemma. Wait until they see the revolt if centrally controlled health care is passed. If you think 2,500 pages in your new policy (as opposed to the 50 to 100 you now have) is a lot, you ain't seen nothing yet. Why are the Noisemakers implementing this system? They are creating it in order to fundamentally change something. They must destroy what currently exists: our capitalist system. Regulations can be used to distort and destroy as well as to improve and offer safety.

Thousands of mortgage brokers may not have literally broken the law, but by arranging for non-qualified people to acquire loans, they had a role in our collapse. They were encouraged to do so by Noisemakers desire to acquire power through votes. If you say that part of the American dream is to own a home, and then you provide a way for people to get one, well guess what? This is not a capitalistic approach. It does accomplish the goal of destroying the existing economic system. These politicians and mortgage brokers both violated the public trust and have placed us all at dire risk today. This will happen every time there is a central control through poor regulation and frustrated capitalist incentive. Look at the devestating results of this one regulation meant to guarantee homes to people who could not actually afford them. It almost ruined the entire world. Every time someone or something interferes with the natural capitalist incentive, they hurt instead of help.

It is not to say that it is right to circumvent government regulations, however. When thousands of trusted professionals say, "I will knowingly profit in the short term and allow others to live with the results of my actions down the line," then this level of unaccountability, opportunism and personal greed violates the bedrock values of our nation just as much as government interference in the free economy. It opens the door to the Noisemakers. Bending laws or misapplying them has nothing to do with a sound capitalistic economy or a sound democracy.

Personally, I am interested in all Americans sitting down and taking stock. I would like to see honest dialogue and a surge in civic participation across the country. This book is not about me being right. It is about us as Americans coming together in reasonable debate and renewed scrutiny of our own actions and those of our elected officials.

When my doctor performs a minor operation, he cleans his instruments afterwards. There may or may not be a law or regulation (although I would bet there is). He or she also has the threat of a lawsuit, but the real reason he cleans his instruments is because he is a man of integrity, sworn to uphold life, not risk it. By the way, YOU pay for all lawsuits, not the insurance company. Think about it.

I ask you in all sincerity: How can we as a people claim a government for ourselves, a capitalist economy and democracy, when we take no responsibility for sustaining it in our personal business choices or in our civic actions?

A charming Noisemaker like Obama who is pushing government control of a free-market economy wasn't elected President in a vacuum.

Without understanding the real events and issues at stake, a majority of the voters reacted to what they saw as a personal feeding frenzy by those in positions of financial trust. They were right to be sickened by this behavior, but confused in their choice of remedy.

The root of government or economic problems in a capitalistic democracy is the people. We the people must wake up, because we've been preyed upon by Noisemakers! When I say, "wake up" I mean we have to become conscious of our common political and economic reality. Then, we have to look at ourselves as individuals and evaluate how we are running our financial and civic affairs. Finally, we have to call for and participate in education of ourselves and our children and grandchildren regarding their relationship with a capitalist system. Education consists of two things, information and application. There is no point in just putting a "module" in civics textbooks. We have to have working entrepreneurial labs in every school, elementary to college. The automatic response that we see today when someone has a financial problem is "How can I get the government or a bank or a credit card to fix this problem for me?" That response needs to change across all groups so that the average person is asking, "What can I create that will generate the money or other kind of support I need?" "How can we leverage our skills, barter, manufacture, negotiate and publicize in order to create a solution to our problem?"

For example: Jane and Tom lost their house because they over-borrowed. They are living with his mother in a three-bedroom, one-bath 900sf house. Jane is an unemployed film camera operator, pregnant with triplets and Tom is an out-of-work journalist with a background working with The Food Network.

Here is a typical list of ways they might try to find a solution to their problems:

1. Apply for food stamps
2. Apply for government housing
3. File for bankruptcy
4. Ask a rich relative for a loan they cannot repay
5. Sell blood, plasma and sperm
6. Sell drugs
7. Buy a used mobile home on credit and put his mother in it, then file for bankruptcy

Here are some entrepreneurial solutions:

1. Go get another job. Here is how you get one. Good workers have no competition today. Most people don't get what I am about to tell you.

I lived in Colorado in the early Seventies. I decided I needed a job in the construction industry. I was a reasonable carpenter, but I knew that no one could out work me. I found a location close by that was building an apartment complex. I drove up to the foreman's shack, put on my tool belt and strolled into the shack and declared to the most important looking guy:

"Hi, I'm ready to work, where do I go?"

He said, "Who hired YOU?"

I said, "You did."

He replied, "I don't remember you, when did I do that?"

To which I replied, "Right now."

He laughed and said, "Go to the first building on the right and report to Jim."

I didn't do the normal thing and ask for an application, fill it out and hope they'd call me back for an interview. I never asked how much they paid because I knew I would eventually be their highest paid and most valuable worker. If I wanted to, that is. (Don't get me wrong, I have screwed up royally in the past also.) If I didn't like the people I worked for or the job, I just went and got another; good times or bad. I don't participate in recessions.

When there is competition in our industries, this is possible. When there is none, like in government and unions, it is not. I always got any job I wanted. I had one guy who said they weren't hiring because they couldn't afford it, to which I replied, "Well, you can't afford not to hire me." He hired me. You must follow through on your promise. I never worried I would be out of work. I understood that most people follow the herd and they all do the same thing and get the same results. Today, everyone has a pretty resume, very few can back it up. I would point this out to your potential employer if I were you, but you won't be telling them anything they don't already know. Think about it.

I realize not everyone is me, but I want you to understand one thing: You must believe in yourself. Failure today is caused when a person does not believe in his or her uniqueness and abilities. STOP IT! Many say they had terrible things happen to them when they were young. I am very sorry about it, but you are now an adult and do not have to let it affect your behavior today. The government will not take care of you, they just want to buy your vote and keep you dependent on them.

2.   Create your own job. Sit down and make a list of things you can do and invent. You might never come up with something, but if you honestly apply yourself you will end up with a job or you will create one.

Let's suppose that instead of experience in TV and media, neither Jane nor Tom has a college degree or a highly marketable skill. Let's say that they have been working in retail all of their lives, just making ends meet. Their parents did the same thing. So what! If you show up on time, ready to go to work and actually work hard, you are already ahead of 95% of the population. Just ask employers.

If Tom became an assistant with an electrician or plumber, he would eventually be able to earn a good living and move up to be the electrician or plumber or even start his own business as one. If he doesn't like it, it will work until he develops what he really wants. In the meantime, Jane could become certified to open her own daycare and lease space from a church. She needs to get out into the community and volunteer. This way she meets people. People who know people put themselves in a position to be hired or backed in their own endeavor.

Each problem that we face is unique, and I assure you that each problem can be solved using imagination, enterprise, democratic action and information. The possibilities are endless as long as the person realizes their relationship to a capitalist system.

Noise Check: Chapter 2

1. If you find yourself without a job, what is the first thing you do?

2. Do you feel that your government has let you down? How?

3. What advice would you give a poverty level single mother with no education?

4. How do you think you will change the way you think about your role in government and your place in the capitalistic system?

5. What have you done in your life that you would call entrepreneurial?

6. How have you fallen prey to Noisemakers?

Do you have additional thoughts you would like to share with me about this chapter, or questions? I want to know what you think! Email me at steve@thenoisemakersbook.com.

A rigid economy of the public contributions and absolute interdiction of all useless expenses will go far towards keeping the government honest and unoppressive.

~Thomas Jefferson, letter to Lafayette, 1823

Big Noisemakers:

Corporations, Governments
and
Investment Houses

Noisemakers are contriving to make us hate the corporations while, at the same time, taking huge contributions from these companies so they can control and micro-manage. It is like the corporations are paying to have themselves deconstructed. This is insane. The very regulators themselves think they are doing well and in some instances they are catching bad guys. More often than not, their efforts are counterproductive because they make it impossible for the good guys to succeed through capitalism.

The people in the regulatory trenches have blinders on. They are under pressure to achieve the unnatural and justify their jobs by creating more rules and continually catching more people. They must do this to save their very existence. I mean, what good is a regulator if they don't create more rules? This happens at all levels of business and state, local, county and federal governments. Just look at various state and federal tax codes, security, construction, and insurance regulations. It never ends until it's all gone and then it really gets bad.

I am convinced, however, that the Noisemakers are being manipulative and dishonest in order to promote their own power agendas. They continually conjure distrust to muddy the waters and allow unnatural perversion of a good system.

American International Group, Inc. (AIG) has hundreds of thousands of workers and many of them are salespeople. If you are a salesperson and you get $100 million on, or if need be, off the books, you will get a bonus. If you overachieve, you will make a bonus. That is the incentive of a capitalist system: productive people are rewarded. In a government system, promotions come from mostly unnatural non-producing sources such as how many fines are assessed. It may appear that fines are a good thing, except for the fact that all fines are paid by YOU in some indirect or direct way. So while you are clapping when our corporations or others are fined for some weird technicality, remember YOU will pay. In a government system, there is also a tendency to create more bureaucracy. What better way to promote yourself than to just hire more people to work under you and create your own fiefdom?

To do this, you must make more rules so you become even more powerful and necessary. If you can collect more fines by having vague rules and become more important and make more money, then that is what you will do.

Yes, companies spend a lot of money on corporate meetings: that's what you do in an insurance company, investment company and any other company to educate, motivate, reward and retain employees. The hardest job to fill is a sales job. Eighty percent of a company's revenue is generated by 20% of its sales force. If you don't reward these people, someone else will: competition. Remember? But if your goal is to equalize outcomes so all people appear equal, you unionize so achievement is no longer rewarded, only seniority. The result is the collapse of incentive for the high achiever and the unnatural continually increasing wage for no reason other than time, thereby causing collapse. Like GM maybe[1]?

The same is true with good corporate chiefs. They are a rare breed and hard to find. You must pay them a lot. Bill Gates is worth exactly what he has. However, as stated before, some of these folks have become more of a political animal than a business person. They crept up the ladder by hook and by crook and not necessarily by achievement. They are political animals. The nose takes on a distinctly brown tint from unknown sources. Many of these folks could not run a convenience store and make a profit. I apologize to all convenience store owners. You actually know how to make a profit and do quite nicely. I was traveling on a Continental flight one day and met a very nice lady who worked for them. After our get acquainted session, I asked her about working for Continental. She loved it. She talked about how great they performed and how great the CEO was and so on. Finally, I asked her why she thought the CEO was so great. She said, "When he walks into a room, he stands head and shoulders above everyone in intelligence."

I then asked a simple question, "Then why is Continental losing money?"[2] She was stunned, speechless. The conversation stopped. I watched as the wheels turned to find an answer.

She finally replied, "I don't know." The rest of the trip was quiet. She was reading a book, but never turned the page for the rest of the two-hour flight. So why was this guy CEO? You tell me. No, I'll give it a shot. Illusion and baloney. Simple as that.

When these folks became the top dog, many put their buddies on boards of directors and approved themselves cash bonuses. This is a misuse of the public trust and it should be addressed without demonizing corporations as a whole. I don't mind these folks being incompetent, however, because it creates competition from the "little" guy. Entrepreneurs are by nature opportunists who look for inefficiency and cure it. They build a better mousetrap. Central control and the lack of capital stifle this ability and corporations become bureaucracies with competing departments that cause the corporation to self-destruct. The CEO then runs to the government for interference and the regulation it needs to unnaturally eliminate any newcomers. They go along with the Noisemakers for self-interest and survival and the gears become gummed up. They fail, or wait, I forgot: They are too big to fail. Baloney! In reality they have opened the door to the Noisemakers for complete control and manipulation. This drags down the good companies with the bad all to the delight of the controllers.

Other things executives get as bonuses are stock options. This is part of the so-called "huge compensations" the Noisemakers are so against. If you are a corporate executive, you may have a salary of X. If, because of your efforts, the company stock price goes from 15 to 30 dollars you've created a lot of wealth and sold product and added more jobs. It is rational that you share in this gain. In fact, as a stock holder, this is what I want. I would like most of top executives' incomes to be dependent on gain as long as it is done in an ethical way. When an executive does it dishonestly, it creates justification in the public's mind for regulation. It is OK to have simple, easy-to-understand rules that prevent harmful fraud and theft, but they must be thought out in a reasonable manner. When the Noisemakers shout "foul," many times they are distorting what happens during the normal progression of capitalist activities.

Governments

On the other hand, if you believe corporations should not reward employees, it is insupportable that the FDIC spent five million on an employee conference in 2009. In fact, you cannot support it at all since the government is broke. What did they produce? If they were to get any kind of a bonus tied to profit, they would owe us, say about 12 trillion dollars. They are not creating money, only spending our money. Such a conference should never have been approved. It should have been a 25 dollar teleconference. If the Noisemakers had the same standard for the government as they did for corporation, they would have to fire, take over, and jail themselves.

To add insult to injury, the FED spends your money and my money regulating the banking industry. If they were any good at what they do, this whole credit debacle would not have happened. The technology crash would have never happened. When they meddle, bad things happen. You cannot control nature and the capitalist system. If you leave it alone, it will regulate itself. Naturally caused ups and downs are good. Capitalist fluctuations create opportunity. Unnatural fluctuations caused by regulation are usually really harmful to the marketplace and the economy. Interference in the free-market process produces unpredictable outcomes and, if recent history is to be a gauge, these outcomes are devastating. So stop already!

These man-made forces also cause huge advantages and opportunities. The Noisemakers are very predictable, and therefore allow the smart investor to make unnaturally large returns when they are able to understand natural outcomes. This is what we will explore. Let's make money in spite of them, what do you say? Let's peer through the veil and see where the money really is and how we can make ours. If we do this, the system will right itself and we can all lead a more stable, productive and profitable life.

Someone once said, "If you can't beat and change a bad system, what good are you?"

We must be careful right now to keep the capital flowing within the United States. When you attack freedom lovers, they react. They do not take it lying down. Sometimes they even leave. If central control becomes too great, and there is no state competition, entrepreneurs and business people may find haven globally. The country of Moldavia actually had an ad for Americans. They advertised a 5% income tax. Think about it! How can we compete with that? Think about what it would mean to you if you had a 5% tax rate. If you are now going to pay 40% of your money to the government so they can go further in debt, what can't you do? If your income as a small business owner is $250,000 and you have to send a minimum of $100,000 to the IRS, what can't you do? You can't expand and hire two people for $50,000 each. These people could produce more goods and make purchases for their family. You can't hire these people if you live in the United States and pay 40% income tax.

Money is leaving and will leave the country for several reasons: taxes and government interference being the two biggest ways that it is taking a hike across the border. The Noisemakers will respond by someday closing our borders. They are already trying to close them when it pertains to our money leaving.

In the financial investment industry, government regulation of the market doesn't allow the average person to understand what their true investment options are. A financial advisor in the United States can't talk to someone about certain investments unless they are accredited. The average person should be able to find out all the information they need to keep their money and grow it. Without sound and ready advice, they are likely to unknowingly provide their money as another "purse" for the government to empty.

Today, most people in the investment industry are afraid to criticize the regulation of the investment industry. They have been threatened into a corner by the government regulators who toss out huge fines for omitting a sentence in a brochure or saying *and* instead of *or*. In other words, they have two species to shoot, stuff and hang on their trophy walls; the advisor and you. You are the unintended game for them. They get you with the ricochet. (Don't fret; you are in the direct cross hairs of lots of folks.) Most advisors are afraid to step out and speak freely, some don't know what they don't know, and some don't care. Most just put their heads down and resign themselves to making money in a "gray" way.

I will repeat that a nation must be made up of good people, informed people and active people. If we (and I'm including investment advisors and brokers) put our heads down and just try to make money for ourselves, we're all going to keep on losing at a rapid pace. Today, advisors are progressively losing public trust. Government is losing public trust. This is a lose-lose situation. Who will win: you or the Noisemakers?

Stand up. Speak up. Vote, complain, write letters, write bills, and refuse to follow the herd. Think it all the way through. Never stop analyzing. You must figure out not only what they are saying and who is saying it, but what YOU think. Ask yourself, "What will really work?" What works may not necessarily be what you would like, but be objective with yourself about what will really work in a positive way for each issue. Think about both sides. Don't be rigid. Consider. It is your duty in a free society. It's your job.

As it stands now, we must change in the Y generation or we end up with institutionalized minds, money and spirit. Government control has sucked the lifeblood out of Europe and Europe is hoping that we Americans get back where we're supposed to be.

When it comes to light that the health care plan put forward by the Democrats in 2009 to the American people was crafted behind closed doors by three people, then what will the American people do? They can't repeal the plan because it has written into it a clause that we do not have a right to repeal it. Or can we? We the people can craft the kind of society we want to have. If we discover that we were told a process would be open and transparent and it was not, we can repeal the plan. We've all read stories of soviet states or Mexico where there is no incentive because there is no hope and the only thing that pays is corruption. With the kinds of backdoor deals that the US Congress makes in the name of "helping"or in the name of "profit," we have all jumped light years ahead in fast becoming another corrupt state.

Eventually, we will see doctors and insurance companies finding a way to do less and provide less: that's what people do. With our current healthcare system, The Canadian Premier, Danny Williams, came to the U.S. for his heart treatment.[3] The natural progression of an overly regulated healthcare system is that the best people will go away, make a deal with Costa Rica and ship rich people over there. The rest of the population will be stuck stateside having to deal with mediocre care.

The Insidious Industry of Investment House Noisemakers

Most brokers are only sales people. They make money selling products such as mortgage-backed securities. They sell primarily stocks and bonds and tell you that you are a long-term investor and therefore you need to "Just ride it out." (How did that work out for you?) They make it sound good if you buy As and Bs and Cs. They make fees on these but their clients ultimately lose and continue to lose money. A normal broker, a stock broker is a transaction based animal. They don't have responsibility for an account, but they don't tell you that, they tell you that they are your advisor.

Folks, there is a big difference between a wire house *broker* and an *independent registered investment advisor.* Examples of wire house type firms are Merrill Lynch, Fidelity, Ed Jones, A.G. Edwards (or is it Wachovia or Wells Fargo?), Charles Schwab, Smith Barney and others. They sell things, usually only stocks and bonds unless you are one of their elite "private" clients. I had one lady who told me a story that her

Merrill Lynch representative told her she could no longer be his client. He said her account got too low. This guy had actually taken her account from a little over a million dollars to under $600,000 in a couple of years and now she didn't meet their minimum account size so she was kicked out. My neighbor's mom was with the same company. Her account went down $300,000 in the 1990's. How could that happen? You could make money in the 1990's by guessing! He just traded her account excessively and was buying high and selling low.

Unlike transactional brokers, registered investment advisors have a fiduciary responsibility to the client. They must look at the entire picture and make recommendations based on the well-being of the client. I am not saying that some brokers don't do this also, but they do not have the same responsibility as does the advisor.

However, none of these people are created equally in talent. For example, the Merrill Lynch clients felt good as they were losing money because Merrill Lynch is a big company. They think that it is reasonable to think that a company cannot get that big without being very reputable, honest, and do good things for people. They do not know or understand the big company's business model. They have no clue what the words, "transaction based" mean. They have been inundated with great sounding commercials from a gigantic marketing machine. They advertise security. They gather assets. They pay hundreds of thousands of dollars in fines. Look at your portfolio. How did it work out for you? "Stay the course," they say. They advise, "Past performance is no indication of future returns." They have conflicts of interest. For example, they (the company) own their own funds and other funds that do not bear their name. They sell stocks as the offering organization. There is unspoken pressure on reps to sell this. Some of these companies were fined because they sold "top shelf products." In other words, funds that paid them extra commissions. We have a list of fines paid by these kind of firms, and it will astound you.

Now look, I am not saying that all the brokers that work for these companies are bad people; on the contrary, they are usually new people in the business and don't have a clue, or they are seasoned and just comfortable in the corporate world where the name brings in the business. They don't know how the business really works and don't have the desire to know or to grow. They are comfortable. Eighty percent of the people will be this way. Remember the 80/20 rule? Many of the best people use the corporate world as a training ground and move on. That describes me. I was working for a very good not-for-profit insurance company.

I learned a lot about insurance and when they eventually decided to get into the mutual fund business, I learned about the investment world.

My problem was I learned that their funds weren't that good when compared to the rest of the world. I couldn't do that deal. When I think there is something better I will go and get it. If I can't get it, I will invent it. I left the insurance company without really knowing exactly how to be in the investment world as a business, but I felt I knew how to make money. I had a very diverse business background and I wanted to develop something new that would make investors money and give them choices they didn't have. I wanted to include all people, not just the so called, "high net worth" folks. Whether you have 10 or 100 gazillion dollars, I love you. Others gather assets, I gather people.

I became aware that people, whether they were rich, middle class or poor, had very little correct knowledge of what was going on in the investment world. I was able to teach people how to use the system for their benefit and not for the investment companies' benefit. I could point out the myths, manipulations and downright nutty and illogical things that happen in our industry. I could not understand why everyone in the business did not take this approach and I still don't. To build trust in people you have to show them how to think through things so they can make decisions based on fact and not manipulation. I never go down the road of least resistance. I don't sell cars.

If you go to the car dealer, they ask you what you are looking for. If you say an F250 truck, they sell it to you. If you tell your advisor you want this investment or that and they agree with everything you say and tell you how smart you are, you better run for the door. It's not that you don't know some things, but in my experience, most people get their information from the normal channels and a lot of it is baloney. Your advisor is supposed to take time and get to know you and explain how certain investments will work for you. What you don't know is what they don't know. If the broker was like me at the insurance company and has five funds to sell, that broker is required to sell you the five funds he has available. If you aren't buying one or all of those five, that broker is out of there.

The problem today is that most investment companies sell basically two products, stocks and bonds. They tell you that if you have this nice colored pie chart of small caps, midcaps, value, etc., etc., etc. and have the long term bonds, medium term bonds, international bonds etc., etc. and you have the right percentages of each according to the risk profile you filled out, then you will be fine. Sound familiar? How did that work out for you? They call it "asset allocation." I call that "asset dislocation." Your assets were dislocated right out of your pocket. You were told you were diversified when you were only diversified within two asset classes. They also told you that when stocks go up; bonds go down. Sounds good huh! Well if that is true and you are a logical person, then you might just come to the conclusion that if you believe what they said, your portfolio will stay the same. The only hope is if one asset class out-performs, the other declines. Think about it.

In today's market, the FED and FDIC regulate and manipulate our monitary supply and interest rates, causing unnatural fluctuations. In this manipulated market, two of the biggest risks are political and regulatory. This used to be how we analyzed developing countries, but now it is here in the US. Thank you, Mr. Noisemaker! When someone like Alan Greenspan or Ben Bernanke or Tim Geithner start fiddling, then weird and unpredictable things start to happen.

In the late 1990's, Greenspan held the record for destroying more wealth than any human that ever lived with his "irrational exuberance" remark.[1] Congress and the Noisemakers now hold that record with their credit fiddling. Yes it is our own fault by allowing this to happen, but when we as citizens don't understand the capitalist, free enterprise system these folks form organizations and systems "for our own good." When regulators feel pressure and rush through regulations, again; weird and unpredictable things start to happen. My response has never been to throw up my arms and say "Oh well."

I ask myself, "Is there anything we can do to take advantage of these manipulations?" It may not be what the manipulators have in mind, but I keep my eye on the ball, making money for my clients in a legal, ethical manner. Maybe someday they will see the light and become more insightful, but it is very difficult to unravel an entrenched bureaucracy. That's why we should NEVER form another bureaucracy. NEVER! Think about it another way. We have spent billions of dollars on the Department of Homeland Security and the TSA and a guy gets on a plane with explosives in his underpants. If you turn the CIA loose, they will find this kind of stuff, but instead we tie their hands and form another department. (Sit back for a second and think about the type of enemy we are fighting when a man will put explosives there.) My point is that when well-meaning people do things, the true reaction is many times different than they anticipate and they create opportunities in unexpected and expected areas. We must be smart enough, creative enough and nimble enough to take advantage of this. Business as usual will not work. Asset allocation as practiced in the past will not hold up in the future. In fact, it really didn't work that well ever, except in the 1990's when everything worked. How did it work out for you in the 1990's? They make it all sound good by telling you if you follow a certain process you will be just fine. They make money but you don't. I'll bet you had a nice pie chart that didn't theoretically violate your risk tolerance form. In the reality of the last downturn, no risk tolerance form or declaration held up. The process was flawed. Many in the investment business are all tied up with process and lose sight of the objective: duh, making money? Whose butt are they really protecting? Think about it.

Folks like Madoff are not taking advantage of anything except their clients. They are actually stupid. They are marketing plans in empty suits. They make noise. They are not innovative, creative, ethical nor do they exhibit any qualities that are the essence of a freedom-loving capitalist. You don't overhaul, over-regulate and manipulate entire systems because of crooks like Madoff. If you do, you just make it worse.

So where do we go from here? Well, we go to the solutions, or at least we start thinking about creating solutions. We think about action and reaction. We put it all together. Before anyone in any industry can become creative, they must understand their business inside and out. It takes decades. A guitar player must understand his guitar, vocals and other instruments before he or she can create a song. In our society, people think they can invest as a sideline and do well especially if they have access to research online from their discount broker.

The interesting thing is that 85% of mutual funds made up of hundreds of analysts and professionals cannot beat their corresponding index. So you have this special talent.... How did that work out for you? Sorry. I know why you did it. You were frustrated with the returns your broker was getting you. I understand. You were paying out all that money and bad things were happening. So, let's explore the whole world of investments so that you can increase your opportunities, choices and develop real strategies that, by golly, may just work for you. How about them apples?

Transactional brokers at large wire houses don't tell people about a whole other world of investments. At this time, these are:

- Non-traded real estate

- Oil and gas

- Managed futures

- Equipment leasing

- Notes: both secured and non-secured

- Private equity

- Tax credits

What is the magic pill?

There is no magic pill, but there is citizen action and there is diversified investing. At our firm, I give people all of the above choices and one or more of them makes money for them in some sort of way, no matter what the stock market is doing.

Transactional brokers tell you that bonds are the conservative side of your portfolio, yet they know that when interest rates go up, the value of bonds decreases. So now if we are sitting at an inflationary cycle you are pretty much guaranteed to lose value. How conservative is that? Then they tell you that if you hold onto your bonds until maturity you will get your principal back. Oh boy, so if interest rates happen to be at 4% and they go to where they went during the Carter years and the value of my 20-year $1000 bond goes down $118 or so for every 1% of interest rate increase I will have?? What? Then your broker will tell you not to worry. He or she will say that if you hold the bond to maturity you will get your principle back. So while everyone else is making double-digit interest returns, I am still making 4% and no one wants to buy my bond. So why do they tell you this? Welllll ummmm. Maybe they only have two products. Ya think? But it is an approved method. Feel better?

How about this: right now, in January 2010, we can buy senior secured notes today that are at healthy discounts. Normally, a note is a loan that is worth a dollar and you get back a dollar. But today, unique circumstances are forcing the sale of these notes at a discount. So if they are with healthy companies that are paying a reasonably good dividend (coupon), we might just get a good monthly check and still get some appreciation. Does it have any risk? Sure it does. ALL things today have risk. The trick is to diversify risk as well as the investment and take advantage of what is happening today. So logic then would tell you that you would buy bonds when interest rates are........??, Yes, correctomundo when interest rates are high because when they fall the value of your bond goes??? Yep! UP. Now we're getting somewhere.

Now don't run out and try to do this today, because I just made it look easy the same way Brett Favre makes a pass look easy, and it is not. There are a lot of details to know. What we are going to do is explore the different asset classes so that you begin to understand the system better and can team up with a good advisor and develop a portfolio tailored to your goals and needs. This information is for everyone, including the broker. I want our citizens, pundits, brokers, brokerage firms, regulators, and politicians to start thinking about how capital is formed in a free enterprise society so that we move out of the quagmire we find ourselves in, so everyone takes a responsible role in our system. Our brokers have become calloused to their clients' losses. They may know or have good reason to believe the bond market is going to go down, but they've got to sell something. They are out of choices. Hey, it's legal and accepted by regulators.

Consider this: if you have a government bond, who is paying the interest? You are. Your yield is that, minus your tax bracket and inflation. Our government is financed with taxes and borrowing. Bonds are the politicians' method of borrowing. (Do you see any conflict of interest here?) It is in the trillions. Our taxes are not keeping up. China now owns a large percentage of our bonds. Our debt is a huge percentage of the GDP (gross domestic product). Do you think China likes us?

Think about that one for a minute.

Politicians want to keep that money flowing into their pockets in order to keep themselves in power in doing what they do. There comes a point that if we continue to operate this way — taking money from the populace to pay the populace without creating new money, we will collapse. Oh, wait…we have already.

As for transactional brokers, I pointed out earlier, most are not actually breaking the law, but they are breaking our trust. Many investment brokers are so prideful about themselves and what they do, that they are lost behind a thick screen of justification. They will do anything to protect the personal opinion that they have of themselves.

Banks

There are two types of banks: investment banks and traditional banks. The investment banker organizes capital. They may underwrite and sell a stock offering and other investment vehicles. Some of these products have caused us great harm. Traditional banks loan money, distribute cds, savings accounts and checking. They may manage trusts and be affiliated with a broker dealer to sell investment products. Investment banks are being referred to as "Wall Street," I think. They are the demon of the day, I think. Those waters sure are muddy, but much of the criticism is well-deserved. The cure seems to be worse than the problem. Imagine that! It does you no good to jump on the bandwagon to dilute Wall Street. You cannot exist without Wall Street. You are

Wall Street! Traditional banks can help create small business and Wall Street makes them big businesses. You own these banks in your 401k, IRA's and investments. If you jump on the "Dilute-Wall-Street" bandwagon, you sign your financial death warrant and will sacrifice your freedom. The very corporation you may work for depends on Wall Street. Don't let the Noisemakers hand you the gun for your own suicide.

All banks are highly regulated entities. By design, they never give money to those that seem to need it, only to those who already have it and can afford to pay it back. (Don't be mad, this is what they are supposed to do.) I will tell you a better source for money later. Even then, they make it look like a huge favor. I guess everyone needs to feel important. They do this except when forced to do something unnatural to them, such as the role of social engineering foisted on banks by Noisemakers in the business of buying votes. Banks are then blamed for the whole mess.

I don't know why banks do not stand up for themselves. We need corporate leaders with strength. Corporate leaders today are political mice. Today, they have put themselves in a ridiculous position. They are between a rock and a hard place. Most businesses in 2010 are not doing that well, and they need operating money, but the banks are reluctant to loan them money because the policies being created by regulators and Congress are not conducive to profit. The last time they loaned bad money they were taken over, but if they don't do what they are told, they will be fined, which means they will have less money, no profits and their stock will fall and you will not invest in them and the government will take them over again, Whew! The lesson here for banks is clear. DO NOT BOW TO PRESSURE FROM THE NOISE-MAKERS IN THE FIRST PLACE! You have PR departments-use them to educate!

Noisemakers find illogical ways to stimulate the economy. They, with the willing help of banks, have established a credit card system that rapes and pillages the poor and the middle class. They even target our kids. Credit card applications to college students now offer a 32%[5] interest rate. These kids have no income. Do you see a problem here? Banks encourage people to spend up to the limit on their card. The result is that they invite more regulation and destroy trust in a free enterprise system. Come on Mr. and Ms. Banker; Let's just do it right. In the long run, it is much easier. Compete on a higher level, you won't regret it. Think it through for our sake and yours.

The PBS show, *The Secret History of the Credit Card*[6] shows how the credit card industry was a conspiracy by those in the government with the willing help of banks to make the economy grow. Government employees sat down and invented the credit card system so the economy would "grow" and so that the politicians would then look good. It was all done with borrowed dollars. It had to catch up with itself at some-time and we are starting to see it today. How well did it work out for you? The point is that we are a nation of irresponsible spenders. We spend more than we make and pay out the nose in interest. When we can't pay, we default on our loans. There is less money for investment and job creation. The US government also spends more than its income. Our debt is out of control. When it doesn't have enough to pay its debt, the government will default. We will essentially be owned by China and others. That's the truth. I can't imagine how bad this might be. It is beyond comprehension.

Don't get me wrong, sometimes debt or leverage can be used to our advantage as long as it is used within reason. I will get to that later. When we complain, we have to remember that we are the government. We still live in a capitalistic democracy. We still have the power to create candidates, write bills, vote and protest. We can still control our own spending. We can teach ourselves and our children how to think as entrepreneurs rather than as institutionalized government payers.

We've been shot and stuffed by the Noisemakers, but it's not too late. Any time you want to stop victimizing yourself, you can. We must put in place people who will stop government spending. It is as simple as that. Noisemakers will promise they will do this, but they will not, they cannot. You must decide who these people are. Think it through. Don't pay attention to who is saying it, but who is doing it. Pay attention! Wake up! Anyone can say anything on the Internet, and you must be able to muddle through the mess and decide what makes sense.

The only promise that comes from a centrally organized system is waiting for your turn in an ever-decreasing marketplace. It is why America outperforms the rest of the world. We are going backward right now. We are sliding downward toward the European method or model that will only lower everyone's standard of living. Europe is starting to riot in the streets for lack of jobs. Where did your money go? Go get it back.

Noise Level Check: Chapter 3

1. What sort of investment advice have you received recently? Do you think that it was good advice? Why or why not?

2. How have you observed regulations interfering with the free market process?

3. What does your neighbor, church friend and/or family member think about the overuse of government regulations? Have you asked them?

4. What do you think about Noisemakers? Can you identify a few Noisemakers?

5. How are you going to diversify your investments so that they are not tied to the stock market?

6. If you could design a system of credit for yourself and others, how would it look?

7. How do you think corporations should be treated by the government?

Do you have additional thoughts you would like to share with me about this chapter, or questions? I want to know what you think! Email me at steve@thenoisemakersbook.com

All, too, will bear in mind this sacred principle,

that though the will of the majority is in all cases

to prevail, that will to be rightful must be reasonable;

that the minority possess their equal rights,

which equal law must protect,

and to violate would be oppression.

~Thomas Jefferson,

First Inaugural Address, March 4, 1801

Noisemaker Tactics:

TAXES

The average person today does not realize the relationship they have to taxes. When you buy a new car, how much of that sales price do you think is profit and how much of it goes to taxes? I'm going to tell you the story of a bolt. When I finish, you tell me what percentage of your new car you believe is allocated to taxes.

Let's take one bolt out of the engine of a 2010 Ford F150 pickup that costs $35K. It sounds like a simple little part, but I want to illustrate how much the simplest things cost and then you can take that to the level of a more sophisticated item and see that the costs are even more.

Step one: To make that bolt, a prospecting company had to find an iron ore deposit somewhere and possibly lease land and get the mineral rights to either mine it or to sell it to a mining company. Whether the prospecting company is the same as or different from the mining company depends on the state where it is found and other details, but let's keep it simple. For the sake of illustration, we will say that the prospecting company is separate from the mining company. So the prospecting company probably had to get permits, permission from landowners, follow state regulations, pay EPA fees, research, pay legal fees and pay federal income taxes. On the tax side, they had to pay employee social security, state income tax, maybe a state franchise tax and safety fees. Each employee had to pay their income tax, social security tax, Medicare tax and if they owned company stock and sold it and there was a gain, they paid capital gains taxes.

We are not talking about normal business expenses here, only the taxes and government fees. There are probably many more that I have not named, because of various state differences and some federal fees and taxes that I don't even know about. Texas, which is one of the most tax-friendly states, has 21 different taxes that may or may not apply. They are online for anyone to review (www.window.state.tx.us/taxes). They even have a tax called a "retaliatory tax." Ya gotta love it.

Back to our bolt. Once the prospecting company locates iron ore, the mining process begins. The mining company pays all of its taxes and fees, and the mining company employees pay all of their taxes. Once the ore is mined, it may be put on trucks and train cars to be shipped to a smelting company and the trucking company pays all of their road taxes for every state their trucks traverse. The railroad industry has their own unique fees, but they also have the usual taxes. After the smelting company reduces the ore to raw stock, it is put back onto a train or truck and sent to a company that rolls it out into a bar. The smelting company pays all of the aforementioned taxes again.

The iron bars then go back on a truck or train and are sent to a factory that cuts the threads and stamps the head. I used to work at a factory in Sycamore, Illinois that made drive lock pins and my hat goes off to the men and women who can work producing "things" day in and day out. You are extraordinary! The bolt is then shipped (tax again) either to Detroit or maybe even to Mexico or Brazil where it is put into your truck in a manufacturing facility. Your truck is then put on a train and shipped to your hometown dealer. That car dealer has to pay all of their taxes including property taxes. Finally, they sell the car or truck with the bolt in it to you and you pay sales tax and licensing fees. It is impossible to make this entirely accurate without months of research, (if you could do it at all) but you get the picture. So after our bolt's little journey, how much of that bolt or truck cost is tax?

When you hear someone say that this group or that company or industry isn't paying their fair share of tax, you may just have a different outlook on things. The only payer of taxes is YOU.

BULLETIN!! Corporations pay no taxes; it is all paid by you because they must pass the costs along. The best thing that could happen to us is that they don't tax businesses at all. Don't hold your breath. Don't forget, that to the Noisemakers, corporations are the incarnation of the devil himself and it doesn't seem to matter that your livelihood comes from their labor, equity and profit.

The Tax Life of a Bolt

1.   Prospecting company (PC) finds an iron ore deposit.

2.   PC leases land with mineral rights to mine or sell.

3.   PC obtains permits, permission from landowners, adhere to state regulations, pay EPA fees, research legal history of use in area, pay legal fees and federal income taxes.

4.   PC pays employee ss, state income tax, state franchise tax and safety fees.

5.   Each employee pays income tax, ss tax, medicre tax and possibly cap gains tax.

6.   Mining company pays taxes and fees.

7.   Mining company employees pay taxes.

8.   Mined ore is put on trucks and train cars to be shipped to a smelting company.

9. Trucking company pays road taxes for every state they traverse. Railroad has unique fees and usual taxes.

10. Iron bars are shipped to a factory that rolls bar stock into long rods.

11. Smelting company pays all of the federal, state and employee taxes again.

12. Iron bars are shipped to a factory that cuts, threads and stamps heads.

13. Truck and train companies pay taxes, and factory pays all taxes.

14. Bolt is shipped to a car manufacturing facility. All taxes apply to shipping company and to car manufacturer.

15. Car is shipped to a hometown dealer who pays all of their taxes including property.

16. You buy the car and pay sales tax and licensing fees.

The biggest part of everything that we buy is taxes, compounded exponentially. Think of everything that you pay in your income and Social Security tax and property tax. I won't even try to consider the taxes that you are paying if you live in California or New York.

Ask yourself, "Are we paying enough to centralized government?" Ask yourself, "Why do I have to vote on raising taxes?" "Why isn't there enough money to accomplish what needs to be done?"

What does this level of taxation do to the economy? Think about the enormity of the tax situation: Military people pay tax on income that all comes from tax money. So do government employees. So, you pay them and then they give part of it back. Sound convoluted? That extra tax money goes to pay for the extra accounting necessary to pay and reroute the paycheck monies back into the system. If we start looking a redundancy and overspending in the federal government, then we will just have to sit down and cry.

Who got shot, stuffed and hung out to dry?

You get stuffed and hung out to dry because you buy food, furniture and transportation. Do you think your income taxes are high enough? If you think they are too high, what can you do about it? What will you do about it? You think about it and I'll come back to it later.

In a 401k, for example, dollars are creating themselves out of nothing. Investment is a form of entrepreneurial activity, but any form of capitalism creates money. Ideally, we would take as much of the money that we create as possible and reinvest it to create more money for ourselves and those who work for us and those whose industries are dependent or peripheral to ours. For example, if Ben and Jerry's Ice Cream were to close all of their retail ice cream stores, the manufacturer of little tables and chairs, the manufacturer of ice cream counter freezers and the real estate leasing agent would all lose business and the people who depend on them, such as plastic molders, would lose business.

When the government passes a bill to hire itself to build highways across the country, how much of that stimulus money actually makes it back to the general population after the government strains it through regulators? The government has no incentive to deliver anything at all to you. The true incentive of government is to make itself bigger. It is the nature of government to infringe upon the rights of the people and it is the duty of the citizen to monitor and restrain government.

People say, "I don't mind paying more to make sure other people have health insurance." My response to that is, this sounds really good and appeals to our very nature to help, but the truth is that the only true way for you to have affordable healthcare is by it being provided through a competitive capitalist system. You don't need to pay any more. No one is turned away at the hospital door, not even people who are illegal.

As for socialized medicine, I promise you that you will not like the intrusion and loss of freedom that will have to occur in a state-run system. In a government system the patient is a liability and a drain on limited resources and in a capitalist system you, the patient, are an asset. The doctor, hospital and insurance company view you as a customer with money that they must compete over. In the state system you use up precious funds and there is no return for you.

You can own the stock of the hospitals and insurance companies; in fact, you do in your 401k. How's your stock in Medicare doing, by the way?

When a politician says, "We're going to help the middle class" I cringe. Why? Because singling out the middle class is a way of demonizing the wealthy and the poor. What is wrong with helping the poor and the rich people? Why don't you help everybody? The middle class cannot grow without the entrepreneurs who come out of the lower and upper class. Why demonize the group that is creating most of our jobs? Most of our country is made up of small businesses. When the Noisemakers focus on the middle class, they take attention away from capitalism as a solution and put it on centralized government as a solution. One group of people cannot benefit from another getting hurt. So why do they do it? Votes maybe?

"Rich who don't pay their fair share..." is another favorite phrase of the Noisemakers. We know that the top five percent are paying 70% of the taxes[1]. I am now in the top five percent, but it wasn't that long ago that I was not. I made other people successful by creating businesses and providing others the opportunity to make a living. The more I am taxed today, the less job creation I can accomplish, I become discouraged and I just don't feel like it. Why should I or any other small business owner work our butts off just to give our profits to the government to do things that just don't work? I built something that didn't exist before with money that didn't come from any other group of fellow Americans.

This manipulation by the Noisemakers creates the kind of economic death spiral we are in in 2010.

By convincing the people that they need to empower government even more, Noisemakers create more power for themselves and do not help anyone. In fact, we all lose financially, politically and we lose personally because we've been duped by people we trusted and elected. Our spirit is wounded and our incentive is down the proverbial drain. Nothing good comes out of this for the citizen, only the elitists in Washington and in our state capitals prosper. If you look at Europe, there is no entrepreneurial wealthy class. Europe is socialized and Europe is in the tank.

When I built my current business I didn't take out a loan. I was lucky I didn't have to. With many small businesses they simply must. I have a line of credit but I use it sparingly. Some projects are just too big to not use it, but it is my last resort. In the upper tax brackets, a small business owner must pay back each dollar earned with $1.40 or more because of federal, state and local taxes he or she must pay on their profits. There's no incentive there to grow and earn more. It's the opposite, in fact.

I make it sound like life has been a bowl of cherries for me, but it has been anything but. I have made almost every mistake that a human being can make so please listen to my mistakes so you can make some new ones. I started out without any money at all, as I told you in the last chapter. I went from scrubbing floors in the airport, building houses, running heavy equipment, doing demolition work, being a railroad signalman, a field engineer, climbing telephone poles in the cable TV industry, to running a bar while playing in various rock-n-roll, country, and even a Mexican band in the 60's 70's and 80's. I held even more jobs than that, but I ran out of breath.

I did borrow money to buy the bar and a truck or two in the cable industry. I thought it would be great to run a bar and play in a rock-n-roll band at the same time. This was in the 70's. Bad idea, especially for me! I had way too much fun, but not much profit! I soon went under and had to file for bankruptcy. This was an unbelievably horrible blow to me. I was only about 21 at the time. I felt like I was a complete and total failure and I would never be anything. It took a long time to get over it, but it taught me a healthy lesson: Be careful and pay as you go if at all possible. From then on I tried to make money first and then expand. It served me well. I know a lot of business people who have extravagant plans and implementation schedules and borrow to do the deal. I know people who have been in business for years and have never made a profit. My rule: Make money first.

After that, I got a job building houses in Colorado. Everyone from Iowa was moving to Colorado because there were no jobs in Iowa. I never thought about it at the time, but this was when Iowa decided to institute a state income tax increase. I just thought that people were moving because Colorado was cool. Colorado was having a boom. It was fabulous! Soon my buddy and I became contractors and we were able to get contracts without getting loans. My philosophy is that a person should always be ready and looking for opportunities. You have to also be prepared for the opportunities and you have to act on those opportunities. The acting part is novel to many people. To act on an opportunity you must be prepared to take risks and in the beginning you have to risk EVERYTHING. This is why there are very few rich people. Very few people can risk everything. It is psychologically very, very hard. But, if it were easy, everyone would do it and there would be no money in it. Sometimes there still isn't because 80% of the people who try it fail[2], sometimes once, sometimes twice, sometimes numerous times before they make it and sometimes they never do. It may sound self-serving, but we must treat these people like our national treasure, not like evil, nasty, rich people who suck the blood out of their fellow men. Business risk-takers are the folks that make this country great.

In between building contracts, I worked in shipyards and ran bulldozers. The next opportunity that presented itself to me was in the cable TV industry. We were living in Iowa at the time and Iowa City was building a new system. I went to work for a company until the system was finished and learned everything I could about the business. There was a boom going on in the industry and when the company I worked for left for the East Coast, I worked a deal to be a subcontractor. I spliced electronics onto the pole. I also worked putting up cable from time to time. We built systems in Maryland, the Carolina's, Miami, St. Louis, Dallas-Ft. Worth and others.

I learned a lot about different cities, the people in the cities, and employees. Did you know that the first part of a cable TV system is built in the lower income areas, or if you like, "the ghettos?" We built the Overtown section of Miami during the riots[3]. We were advised by the police to carry guns. We did. I only had to pull it out once to discourage a guy with an ice pick. He broke the cardinal rule of the ghetto. Never bring an ice pick to a gun fight. He left in a relatively good mood and we started gaining respect. I mean respect according to their rules, not ours. There were a couple of other instances with our crews, but it soon got around that you didn't mess with the cable guys; they were crazy (whatever works). Don't get me wrong, we were crazy. One of the Mississippi cable guys had a gun pulled on him while he was up a telephone pole. The robber said, "Throw down your money!"

The cable guy looked down, pulled out his gun and said, "F———— you a————, throw up yours." The robber ran. Guess he couldn't afford any bullets. As you can see, the guys that worked for me and the guys I worked around fit the "crazy" bill pretty well. They were from the backwoods in Mississippi. They had names like Shaggy Dog, Flyback, Junior, Kelly Red, Butch, JR, C, Bubba (I don't think Bubba Clinton would fit in as we didn't have any Rhoades Scholars) and the likes. It was party central. We all got paid by how much we did, not by the hour. The money was fabulous if you worked. I learned the lesson that you paid people by what they did and not by the hour. When you do this and hire right, you serve more people and everyone makes more money. It worked great in the construction business. We also got paid by the foot.

You just had to watch quality. If you made someone do some-thing over again because quality was bad, it didn't take long to make your point. They couldn't make any money if they were fixing their mistakes. An hourly person has less incentive and there is less downside for mistakes. I'm sure you've heard the expression, "It all pays the same."

These were industries where if you fired someone, you might have to fight them too. I wish everyone had the work ethic of these backwoods men. They may not have been educated, but they were smart, talented, they took care of each other and they could outwork anyone if they so desired. I have a lot of respect for these kinds of folks. They are genuine people and they will watch your back if you can gain their respect. They don't play games and tell you what's on their minds. They make America great. They build it. Everyone needs everyone else in this country.

I see the people in Washington playing these people down and disrespecting them, by manipulating them and lying to them for their own political gain. These hardworking people should be able to trust their leaders and they can't. You don't need to do anything for these folks, but get out of their way and provide a pro-business environment so they can work. They don't want a union; because they know it will only hold them back. Union workers get paid by the hour and their raises only come from seniority and negotiations which they cannot control. These guys would be shunned as overachievers if they belonged in a union. To get on with my story, even though I made money hand-over-fist building cable TV systems, the business soon became corrupt. People asked for kickbacks and I didn't play that game, so I quit and moved back to Iowa.

In Iowa, I worked on a commercial construction crew, but I was not making ends meet very well. I was paid by the hour. It was hard to be working for someone else after running my own business and making much more money.

One day, a lady came to my house selling life insurance. I told her I wanted to sell insurance too. After an hour or so of discussion she said, "You need to talk to my boss."

The boss said, "You need to take tests."

I took tests.

He said, "You're not qualified to work for us. The tests say you're not the personality style nor do you possess the attributes that we're looking for. You'll fail in the insurance business. You don't have the skills that will allow you to succeed."

I calmly thought, "WRONG!" I said, "Hire me and I'll be the best producer you ever had in your entire career."

He had to go up the ladder to get permission to hire me. I give him a lot of credit for bucking the system. He took a big risk for a corporate world manager. If I had failed, it would have gone badly for him. The boss gave me half of the initial survival money that they regularly pay new salespeople to ramp up to a 100% commission status. He also gave me an underdeveloped territory. No one had ever succeeded in the area he gave me.

Within one year, I became the number one producer in A territories in the entire country. I stayed number one, and they made me a District Manager. I really was tired of Iowa, and of my boss. The better I performed and the better my group performed, the more he tried to control me. My group per individual was outperforming his. I could spend quite a good amount of time on the psychology of that, but who cares? I'm glad he was like that. Otherwise I might have stayed and that would not have been good for me.

Many corporate home office people have a distrust and disdain for high producers. They look at a high producer's pay and compare it to their salaries and something happens in their minds like, "We're the smart ones up here that make things work, we should at least get what they do out there in the field so......Let's cut their commissions. Yeah, that's the ticket, then they'll have to work twice as hard to make the same money."

They actually cut our commissions in half! This is what big corporations do. They determine what they want to pay their sales force and when they achieve it, they cut their commissions to keep corporate costs the same and improve profits. This is a very shortsighted, non-entrepreneurial practice. Having said that, I am thankful that they do this. Losing half of my commission was part of the reason that made me leave my comfort zone and move on. What does that say about the ones who stayed? Don't get me wrong, we need the corporate world and many are comfortable there, just not me and maybe not you. Large corporations provide the training for the entrepreneur to learn a craft or business so they can create a better mousetrap and the world can keep growing and improving. Entrepreneurs actually keep our big corporations honest.

Note: An entrepreneurial spirit could have happened in the banking industry and may have averted the credit crisis and our near collapse, but regulatory costs make it virtually impossible to create the competition we need to keep us from having the next fiasco. Local banks weathered the storm much better than the big ones. In fact many are cruising along just fine.

Competition is capitalism. It forces everyone to a never-ending higher level of achievement and prosperity. It will weed out inefficiencies and cut costs that will be passed onto you, the consumer, which keeps our economy chugging along. So I am thankful for my corporate friends and have the highest level of respect and I apologize ahead of time for putting you out of business......Just kidding! I think. Well, maybe not.

As I said, I was getting itchy feet for various reasons and I got a call from the Texas General Agent who said he was going to retire soon and wanted to go out as the number one agency in all three territory types: A,B, and C. He already had the top B and C but not A. Would I come down and work with him? He was a character. He was from the old guard and not part of the "new" corporate "whatever it was." He said he would pay my way. My General Agent was not too happy, but he had to give in. He did so gracefully and I moved to the greatest state in the country. WOW! I could not believe the positive business climate and the affluence!

Texas should be the model for the rest of the country. It has low taxes and entrepreneurial freedom. Iowa had a top income tax bracket of 9.98% and Texas had zero. (Remember the tax death spiral.) My house was free because of the tax savings. You do have to be careful though; Texas has a little bit different way of doing things and some folks have a little problem with ethics. I was used to the Iowa farm boy ethics and Texas has the Oil Patch. You just have to know people better here.

The regulators are still doing their thing that they do and we are following the regulatory progression to the dark end, it's just that we here in Texas fight a little harder. I came from Iowa, and I love it, but at heart, I am a Texan. I love the free spirit and independent thinking that goes on here. I'm glad my kids grew up here. Oh, and it's warmer here and they don't have Blue Marlin in Iowa. Every summer I return to catch a few catfish or bass with my brother Dave on the Mississippi River and go to the Fort Madison Rodeo, eat some Maidrites at the little Maidrite shop, and gobble up a couple of pounds of Sterzing Potato Chips.

As I settled down to life in Texas, I thought to myself, "There's a whole big investment world out there that I can't offer my clients as a life insurance salesperson." My company had about five or six mutual funds that were not very good. I would go to bed at night wondering about how ethical it was to sell someone a product when you knew of others of the same kind that were better. The only way for me to grow, and serve my clients in a way I thought was ethical was to go into business for myself. If I were a car dealer I would want to sell all cars if I could, or at least pick what I thought was the best. If I was to sell investment products, I wanted to find the best and expand the diversification horizons. That's what I wanted for myself, why wouldn't I want it for my clients? You know, it is easier to do it right than to do it wrong. This is a lesson that crooks like Madoff don't get. The straight way is really the easy way, because you always reap what you sow.

I quit my job with the life insurance company. I had no clue what I was going to do. I didn't know how, or where, to start looking. A friend of mine also took the same path. He found a broker dealer that catered to independent representatives and we made the move.

I loved the freedom and product choices. It was great. I felt confident I had developed a common sense, no nonsense approach I was proud of. My wife ran the office and developed the office procedures and operations. I owe everything to her. I am not a paperwork, detail-type person. I am a creative concept person that sees the whole picture. I can implement the concept but I don't enjoy the small tasks. She is good at thinking through and making it all work together and I can trust she won't drop the ball and she never forgets anything. She can remember what happened on December 4, 1990 with a $3K client. It's amazing. The best functional marriages seem made up of these opposites. It's a team deal. Common wisdom says find someone that is like you with whom you have a lot in common. From my work with people and their finances over the last 24 years, I find the opposite to be true. One needs to make up for the other's weakness as we all strive towards balance. One is usually a spender and one is a saver. News flash! Both of you are OK. You can develop a "spend it all budget" that will make both of you happy. Ask me about it sometime.

It took us about three months to get the new business going and within a year, we were earning over the six-figure mark and kept moving up the ladder. Clients were making a lot of money and so were we. It was the 90's and things were fabulous. I was a broker as well as a

Registered Investment Advisor. Most people are one or the other, but I thought it was a good idea to develop a model that would eliminate any conflicts of interests, biases and to have no proprietary arrangements. This is rare in the business. I do not understand why everyone doesn't do this. My company is a Registered Investment Advisor, which means that I have fiduciary responsibility for my clients.

The typical stock broker at a big wire house is just making money by buying and selling things for a commission. These are transaction based people. They make money when a trade is made. They are not responsible for the results in an account, but they have regulations they must follow such as suitability, know your client, and others. Brokers are not bad people, they are just different than what the normal person thinks. They gather assets and sell things. OK, I am also a broker. Remember what I said, I wanted no conflicts or biases. Sometimes it is better to buy on commission and sometimes not, but most people in the business only do one and then convince you their way is the best.

Registered Investment Advisors (RIAs) will tell you that their way is best because their income is tied to yours, so when you make money, they get a raise. They have an interest in seeing increasing values. But wait! They also charge you if it goes down and they will tell you that they must work harder when times are bad. Both statements are true.

RIAs gather assets also. In fact they even advertise that fact and the industry judges them on it. They advertise a phrase like, " 50 BIL-

LION dollars under management" and you are supposed to be impressed and do even more business with them. This sort of marketing worked for Madoff, but not for his clients. We are asked how much we have under management all the time, usually by magazines, newspaper reporters and others in the business.

I do not disclose the number because it is totally irrelevant. My reply? "We don't keep track of our assets under management. We keep track of our clients' assets." When you gather assets under management, you generate recurring income and you have a tangible asset to sell someday. Think about it! What about returns? Unfortuneately, RIAs can't tell you the return they make because, if they did, they would have every regulator in the world in their office trying to shut them down. It would be impossible, anyway, as every client should have a different return because there really should be very few people with the same account when you look at things like economic conditions, market conditions, timing of such, availability, new products and many other facts. They also can't have any endorsements. This is illegal and most wise advisors are scared to death to even give references for interpretation reasons, it's just too risky. Besides, when it comes to confidentiality, most folks are quiet about their money. Many advisors will ask for referrals aggressively. I just try to shut up about it and figure if folks want to tell someone, they will, and I will just keep doing what I do and it will work out. It does. For more information, I suggest you go to the Financial Planning Association's Web site (www.fpa.org) and study the differences between various RIAs.

So which is better: commission or fees? Neither is better. It depends on the circumstances of the investment at the time. If I think I will hold an asset for, say, five years, should I pay a commission or a fee? Let's see. If the commission on some mutual fund that I put $100K in (just an example, don't get excited) is five percent and I hold it for five years and it grows to $200K, then I paid $5K or I actually invested $95K, but that's all I paid. If I paid a two percent fee per year, then I paid $2K the first year and increased that amount the second (if it made money) and even more the third, fourth and in the fifth year I paid $4K. So just between the first and fifth years, I paid more than the total of the commission and that doesn't even include the years in-between.

However, if you trade around a lot for whatever reason, it may be more beneficial to pay a fee. Fees are negotiable by the way, but if someone gives you a cheap fee, they are telling you something....Hmm. Yep, they're cheap maybe? Note: never deal with a cheap, broke financial advisor. When it comes to fees or commissions, I just talk about the account and how it works and I let the client decide. They might even have both. Some of the more sophisticated products we will discuss have internal fees and your investment is not reduced directly. Here, a fee makes little sense most of the time. It's all marketing anyway, folks: A shares, B shares, C shares, P shares, load funds, no load, and front-end load. Jeez who knows? None of it matters. It's all about load adjusted return. Surprise! No one works for free! In other words, at the end of the day, after all fees and commissions are paid, how much do I have in my pocket? If someone is competing on fees, they must not be too concerned about quality.

I am a risk-taker, but I do not consider myself a gambler. I trust my inner self, but I have a healthy skepticism. I am never All-In. I leave an Out. I don't trust people in general, but they can change my mind during our relationship. I think folks are mostly good, but have a hard time understanding ethics in today's complicated world. Some become bitter and will stray from the path when they are desperate or in a bind.

The bigger the corporation, the more the relationship between it and the customer becomes separated. The two sets of goals do not gel. The less personal, the more the customer is commoditized and the more the company looks to profits before service and benefits for the customer. I position myself to fill the gap. If we have a personal relationship with the client first, eliminate bias, conflicts of interest, and be careful about with whom we affiliate, the better it is for the customer. If we do not restrict our opportunities for product and diversification and keep a keen eye on innovation with a healthy skepticism, then we will continue to flourish because the customer is flourishing and not the other way around.

It is actually easier to keep the customer uppermost as a concern than not. To be in the investment business and only have the ability to use two products seems insane to me. At least if that is what I am going to do, I should disclose it. Many brokers do not disclose the fact that they can only represent two or three products. You suffer as a result and the industry suffers. You lose money and become disillusioned and put your money under the mattress and fewer and fewer jobs are created.

I want to see credibility return to the investment business by increasing your faith and creating an ever-increasing economy and wealth for all citizens of the world. To do this, those of us in the investment industry, including regulators, need to punch the RESET button in a few areas. These are: Regulation, ethics, responsibility, citizen involvement and education of fact and history.

I am a solutions guy and we will discuss how this "reset" can be done in upcoming chapters as we talk about how you can better survive in today's world, make money, and even thrive. We must all work to revamp the investment side of the economy together. No other country can do this, only the United States and only because of you, the United States citizen.

The solution I suggest has two parts: 1) Demand that the government detach itself from private enterprise where it has been feeding like a great leech. 2) Generate more wealth through greater entrepreneurial activity by thoughtful, studied action on the part of United States citizens.

The government acts as a leech in ways that are often unobserved or ignored by the average person. For example, when I was in the cable business, cable was a new, booming, industry. All the new systems had to be built, and there was a lot of money flying around. This sort of boom invites corruption. Instead of allowing for competition, national, state and local governments decided to get a piece of the pie. Individual politicians received bribes. This was BIG money. The result is what you see today. You probably have one cable system in your community and they negotiate with your local politicians for rate increases and contracts. How is that working out for you?

Once they deregulated the electric industry, we were allowed to purchase through different companies and the price of electricity went down. What do you think would happen if you had more than one cable company? What if we went from many insurance companies for our healthcare to one and that one is trillions of dollars in debt? How about being able to buy our insurance from any company we want instead of just the ones in our state?

I don't really need to give you the answer do I? If I do, you are not thinking. This book is about thinking. The solution to our financial problems in this country is as simple as you making a choice to focus your attention on those problems in a systematic way. You must become engaged in a process of logical thinking. Listen, engage, process, decide, be flexible, and weed out the baloney. Get it?

Form small groups of your neighbors, talk about things. Form small groups at church. I suggest you read Rick Warren's book, *A Purpose Driven Life*. Step out of your comfort zone by including people who are not like you in the discussion group. Learn how to think through financial and political choices. Ask, "Why is this happening? What do I know and what do I not know?"

I said to associate with people that are different than you, but I want you to be careful who you choose as mentors and support people. As I grew and evolved as a businessperson and as a politically aware citizen, I wanted to find people who were doing better than I was and then I wanted to do better than them. I continually read books, went to coaching seminars, motivational gatherings and tried everything I could think of to improve myself and my situation in life. I wanted to improve as a person. I believe God wants me to do things, but I don't know exactly what they are, so I am prepared for what happens, no matter what it is. I try to take advantage of every opportunity. Sometimes I am a reluctant warrior, but I have learned to just do it anyway and shut up.

For instance, I was given the skills and experiences to do interventions for people who have drug and alcohol problems and so I do them. I don't want to do them, because you must deal with ugly, evil things, but I must. Addiction is a disease of the spirit and must be dealt with as such. From my perspective, when I look into the eyes of an addicted person, I am not looking into the eyes of the person but into the eyes of the addiction. That is a different entity that is totally disassociated from the true individual.

I feel the same way about everything I do in life. This is how I run my businesses. He, God, gives me positive jobs also. I love what I do in the investment business and it balances out the ugliness of other things.

God never gives me more than I can handle, but He will take me right to the edge. I didn't and still don't always do His will, but I try to always be moving in that direction and I strive to get better every day. I am always where I am supposed to be and doing exactly what I am supposed to do, even if it is dumb and I am supposed to learn a lesson. I feel I am required to be the very best I can be. I am a work-in-progress. How about you?

I was the oldest of seven brothers and sisters in Iowa. My dad worked for a savings and loan. Life with seven kids was tough. Each one of us wanted to be the one sitting next to the chicken plate when the prayer was over. I figured out (as the oldest, of course) that if I helped Mom set the table, I could put that darn plate right next to me. We call Mom "Mean Jean." She is anything but mean, but she ran a tight ship. My mom and dad were busy from morning to night so I sort of raised myself. My grandfather took me duck and squirrel hunting now and then. He lived right on the banks of the Mississippi River and he often let me do my own thing. I would get in the boat and go exploring. I went squirrel hunting by myself, tramping in the woods for days. I wasn't that great in school but I read the World Book encyclopedia by the time I was 12. I loved the way it looked with it's gold trimmed pages and white cover. I still don't understand that. I had some friends, but I never fit into the crowd perfectly. I never fit into any one group totally in my own mind. I could move from one group to another easily. Most people could get along with me and I could get along with them. This was an advantage because I got to learn about a lot of different people. I learned that I had a lot in common with most people. I tried to learn from everyone. I never thought that because I might make more money or appear to be smarter than someone, they could not teach me anything. I got some very wise insights from some of the least educated. I learned to be careful about accepting information from academics. Some seemed to live in a theoretical world that followed a type of linear group think that put them in what I call "the herd." Sometimes it was the world of the absurd.

If you want to excel and create, you have to understand the herd and where they are going and get out in front of it. The herd becomes predictable, and you can use the direction of the herd to take a different course that leads to success. This is how I developed my company's Orrbital Investment Process. This process allows us to stay ahead of the herd by diversifying into eight or nine different asset classes instead of two. The investment world is moving in the same direction we are now, but they are about 15 years behind and will never catch up. My company and my clients continue to grow and evolve towards the future. We are not standing still. We will stay on the cutting edge. We didn't invest in any mortgage backed securities! We used to call our program of diversification, "Core and Satellite investing," but others co-opted the term so we call it "Orrbital." I was a little turned off by Orrbital at first because it sounded a bit arrogant, but gave in to the marketing folks I had at the time and figured it would be an easy way to keep it as our own brand. It is hard to copy a term when it has someone's name in it.

After going through so many experiences, I now have so much respect for entrepreneurs. Most people don't realize what they go through to succeed. Our schools should have a mandatory class on entrepreneurship that tracks a business through the regulations, fees, expenses, money raising, marketing and all the craziness business people must endure. The Americans with Disabilities Act requires that businesses have all toilet paper dispensers, door handles, and entrances just so.

The local folks will regulate even how tall your bushes should be and what kind you can have and whether or not they like it. The interesting thing is if you go to the government buildings, they are the biggest offenders of their own regulations. The local ordinances and federal regulations are thousands of pages long. It is a miracle when a new business is formed today. There are few incentives left. Our regulatory and tax systems discourage the little guy and make us more susceptible to monopolies. When small businesses do finally make it, they are monetarily rewarded. They then become prey to the government again. They are labeled "the evil, wicked rich folks" who have led lives of privilege or who "got lucky" in the lottery of life and owe all the rest of us something in the form of higher taxes etc. There will only be about 10% to 20 % of us that ever get to this point.

For a Noisemaker to say that the "rich" are a cancer to society, [5] that is simply a strategy designed to pit people against each other in order to gain power and to buy votes. If they can get us all dependent on them, then everything will be as they want it, i.e., they will control wealth, production and spending.

Remember that I mentioned how my cable team, back in the Eighties helped set up cable in Overtown, the lowest income section of Miami, first? At the time, the Overtown riots were occurring. I understand the frustration of people living in a place such as Overtown. The Noisemakers, however, have convinced black people that the right-wing built the ghettos to keep them in their places. The Noisemakers are the people who actually built the ghettos and are the ones who blamed it on the nasty rich people. What incentive do the rich people have to keep the black people marginalized in ghettos? In fact, it is the opposite.

By keeping blacks marginalized in ghettos, the Noisemakers have fewer entrepreneurs, fewer customers and a sense of urgent despair that they manipulate for their own political gain. If the Noisemaker policies were truly designed to help people, then the ghettos should have gone away. Did they? The constant Noisemaker talk about racism has their desired effect of keeping people fighting each other. Many of the black people I know just want to get ahead. They don't think white people are taking opportunities away from them. They know the truth is that there are people out there who will hire whoever can do a good job. They understand and have embraced capitalism and reject the Noisemaker drivel of destruction. The entrepreneurs of the ghettos are the drug dealers and thieves. They tried to bribe us with cash to get cable first. They had rolls of cash. The rest are struggling to find a way out, but think they can't and in many respects, they are right. Walter Williams writes about this factor in his columns and books[4].

If these folks would follow Williams and Thomas Sowell[5] and their writings, they would soon dig themselves out of where they are and provide opportunities for themselves. I promise that if anyone waits for government to provide a solution for them that works, they will stay in one place forever. Many people who live in the ghettos of the United States clearly understand their relationship to a centralized control system, but they reject the world of the rich and successful by labeling it "white." This keeps them where they are mentally.

There are three rules to success: 1) Have a vision, 2) Get comfortable being uncomfortable and 3) Never quit. If you live in poverty and you have demonized the wealthy, how can you ever even create a vision for yourself? How can you even accomplish step one?

Rich people know that the more money the general population makes, the more money there is for everyone. They are rich because they know that there is not a limited, finite amount of wealth to go around. They realize in a capitalist system, money is created from nothing. The Chinese have figured this out in the last 15 years and now own much of our debt. We are buying more of their products than they are buying from us. They have grown their economy at about 10% a year for the last 10 years and they are just getting started.

Noisemakers are able to convince poor people that the rich are trying to keep them down because that is how poor people think about money: there's a finite amount and they want to keep it all for themselves. They think that money is like a pizza, but it's really more like space. The Noisemakers are playing off of the insecurities of the poor to keep them voting for them. Basically, it's an inhumane power play... and it works.

Noise Level Check: Chapter 4

1. Tell me about some business risks you've taken in your life.

2. How did you benefit from those risks? What would you do differently?

3. Why is there such a large gap between the poor and the rich in the United States?

4. If you could change the US method of taxation, what would you do? Why?

Do you have additional thoughts you would like to share with me about this chapter, or questions? I want to know what you think! Email me at steve@thenoisemakersbook.com

A people... who are possessed

of the spirit of commerce,

who see and who will pursue their advantages

may achieve almost anything.

~ George Washington,

letter to Benjamin Harrison, October 10, 1784

The Golden Parade

of

Unrelated Asset Classes

The question is: How do I take my dollar and create more dollars with it? It sounds like a simple question, but I believe that there is quite a bit of confusion in this country about creating more money. One misconception is, "If money doesn't come from me directly, then it comes from somewhere else." People believe that when they receive money from the government, it is somehow not their own money. I get a kick out of local politicians who proclaim the fact that none of their pet projects used any "local money." I guess it came from outer space. Maybe the Fifth Dimension. In reality if you think about it for half a second, Texas money goes to Washington and then is paid out non-locally. Duh.

Picture a dollar bill. Little and big pieces of it are torn off by various aspects of bureaucracy. Finally, a little corner of that bill is returned to you in the form of a service, subsidy or infrastructure. You receive a benefit and you think, "Oh, I just received something." No, you just paid five times more for something than you would have if you had purchased it directly. The "Cash for Clunkers" program is a good example. Every time you participate in a government program that returns money to your pocket, such as tax credits, subsidized loans or subsidized building projects for greater energy savings, you are just paying yourself in torn up pieces of your own money. Government funds are tattered pieces of your dollars. That is why it does no good for the government to pump money into itself or for them to "invest in you." For us to survive, we have to become savvy on how to get our dollar to multiply in spite of the things Noisemakers do and in spite of what the market in general does. To do this we must look at diversification differently. Not only do we want to diversify inside an asset class, we must diversify into more asset classes.

The most important part of diversified investing is to have multiple asset vehicles that are not dependent on or related to one another. We need not be correlated in our investment program to the extent that we have been. For instance, if one asset class fluctuates downward, it may not affect other investments.

Let's do this in an orderly fashion. First, let's talk a little bit about some of the things you are familiar with: stocks and bonds. Before you or I can even look at the actual stocks and bonds, we have to first understand how the industry works. Investing requires you to choose a broker and/or advisor usually, so you will need to know how to evaluate these people before you follow their advice.

I want to get even simpler and talk about mutual funds, which is the way most people invest today by contributing to them in their 401k's and IRA's. If you want to get information on how to be a stock jock, you can get it elsewhere, because if there was anyone really good at this they would be famous and you could read their book. Eighty-five to 90% of mutual fund managers stink up the place. I'm saying that they are ineffective and… "insincere" would be a good word to use here. So if you think your broker can make a substantial profit investing your money for you while they call 40 people a day and review with another untold number every week, guess again. They are simply too busy. So am I, so I just look for the best money managers out there and hire and fire them as need be.

Guess what! Effectively and honestly managing money so that it creates more money is easier than you think, AND I'll bet your money manager stinks up the place. I know this because I have been looking at portfolios like yours for decades. Believe me…They stink, stink, stink! Uh, did I say they "stink?" Go ahead and try to prove me wrong.

Don't take my word for it. You could use Value Line, CDA/ Wiesenberger, and Morningstar[2] to rate the funds your broker suggested and check their performance, but you would not know how they compare to each other. You say, "Well Steve, I looked at my funds online with a third-party rating system and it looked OK and anyone can do that." Yes, but how did yours stack up against, say, the other growth funds, for example? It's this easy. I have a program that compares all of these funds to one another. I can give the computer numerous criteria and, low-and-behold, they pop up in order of performance. I can even use load-adjusted criteria if I want. (A load adjusted return is the return on a mutual fund adjusted downward to reflect any sales fees, whether front-end or back-end.)

You say, "But Steve, the regulators say past performance does not indicate future return."

My reply is that I'm sure this made sense to say when they said it, but think about it. Secondly, your transactional broker does not explain all of the various types of funds and investments that are performing well because, well, they don't have them to sell.

They are transactional brokers. This means that they sell things. Why not sell you their company mutual funds above all others? They know you trust them and they know you will not take the time and energy to research all of the 17,000 mutual funds available and compare their yield rates, nor do you have the tools. Some may actually be sincere in the belief that their funds are good, but their funds are not good. These folks don't have the tools or the desire to do comparative fund research. So they sell you their own poorly performing funds and they make a fee or commission from the sale. They make their employer happy and keep their job.

Many wire houses that own their own mutual funds are so respected in the industry that people feel irrational comfort in investing in those funds. I say, irrational because it is irrational to put all your money into investment vehicles that have gone nowhere and have a poor track record. You are also told that you are a long-term investor and I want to remind you that the only thing long-term about your investment program is that you have a long life and will be investing throughout that entire period. Thinking of yourself as a long-term investor is irrational. Sure, the big brokerage firm may have nice commercials, a posh office, all your friends go there, your broker is handsome and seems to be smart. You may feel as comfortable as a worm in an apple, but that doesn't mean that you're not losing money hand-over-fist on a regular basis! It doesn't mean that your 401k isn't garbage. Every person who ever came to me from one of the big wire houses had poorly performing funds. Prove me wrong!

Take a look at a third-party rating system. Compare your funds with others listed there. A transactional broker at a large wire house is not a financial advisor. They do not have the same fiduciary responsibility as a Registered Investment Advisor. Your trust in them may be unfounded. You are responsible for making sure that you're not being hoodwinked. I am giving you the tools to make good decisions. Some of these wire houses ought to have a big cow instead of a bull as their emblem because they are milking you.

Long ago, someone spit out the phrase, "Past performance is not an indication of future returns." For decades, brokers have been using that phrase to convince investors to buy poorly performing stocks or convince them not to buy those that performed well in the past. That's just crazy. Someone made it a blanket statement and it became distorted and used by Noisemakers. Sure, not every stock, bond or fund that once made money, will again, but by-and-large, past performance is a good indication of future returns. Bankers and brokers who say this to you are Noisemakers who are trying to get you to fit into their marketing plan. They are saying, "Forget about the customers, what can we get for us?" How do they get away with giving you crappy advice? Regulators gave them the laws that encourage them to conform to established practices across the industry. The regulators needed to have everyone appear to be exactly alike. These kinds of regulations don't protect anyone except the Noisemaker bankers and brokers. They sure don't protect you. For instance, Bernie Madoff's multi-billion dollar ponzi scheme passed every regulator without a problem.

The job of a typical transactional broker at a big wire house is to call 30 to 50 people a day to get them to buy stocks. These people are caught in a straightjacket. To survive, they sell new things and tell you to sell and buy NOW whether it makes sense or not. Many don't care what happens to you since they make money either way. They sell two things-stocks and bonds. Oh yeah and brokerage CD's. Whoopi!

That's a quick overview of the investment industry as a whole. Now let's move on to the actual asset vehicles: stocks and bonds.

Stocks

The stock market is one of the most important institutions for job and wealth creation. It has its place in all our portfolios. It can have periods of extreme profitability. It can have decades where it is relatively flat, and yes, it can plummet. Stocks are ownership dollars in contrast with bonds which are loaner-ship dollars. Many people today participate in the market through their 401k at work, others in their retirement accounts such as IRA's. Others participate just as a liquid investment. There are many facets of the stock market and it can be a complex process to even make a profit for most. I say most because 85% of the mutual fund managers, employing large staffs cannot even beat the index by which they compare themselves. The biggest and most popular index is the S&P 500. This is why many managers and advisors recommend index funds. That way you can at least be average. That sounds like fun right? I get to be average. What did your advisor just tell you? Could it be that he is well…..average? One of the largest advisory firms in the country, Eric Edelman, will put you in one of his 43 different portfolios according to the risk form you fill out online. He will then put you in various index funds. Recently, he has begun to put his clients in Exchange Traded Funds (EFTs). These are like index funds in that you own all of a sector: average. These folks compete on low fees. I wonder why?

Let's talk about why the funds in your 401k aren't working for you now. How do you know if you have the best in each category? If you are a 401k trustee, how do you know if you are giving your employees the best possible choices? If you are an advisor, how do you know if you are giving your clients the best? You might say that you are satisfied with what you have, but how do you know you couldn't do better?

Go to a third-party rating system and find your fund and look at its performance and risk rating. How do you know how your fund really stacks up to the others? You don't. Why? You can't unless you are able to use technology the way I have been able to use it and apply 23 years of experience. I can walk through a desert and see only sand. An Indian woman from Mexico's east coast can walk through the desert and identify hundreds of edible plants, seeds and animals. You have to be in the environment for a long time and train yourself to see what is hidden in plain sight.

I have been looking at personal accounts and 401k's for 23 some years now and I can probably assure you that yours stinks. I can tell you that if you are with Edward Jones you probably have American Funds. I think that Edward Jones was fined for selling those as top-shelf prod-ucts. In other words, they were paid one percent extra to sell these. They admitted no wrongdoing and I am sure they were cooperative — to the tune of about 80 million greenbacks. If you are with Merrill Lynch, you may just have funds that are owned by Merrill Lynch. The bull or the bull: You decide. If you want a list of fines paid by these people, Eric Edelman put them in his book, The Lies About Money. If you want to know about the fines, they are public record. I think I have a list current to about 2007. I'll send it to you. You'll get the picture.

In fact, if you want to be average, you can even go into one of his cookie cutter strategies. One only needs to go online to access this information, or you can keep reading here and be above average or maybe even thrive. I want you to know as much as you can about how the industry works so you can make an informed decision for yourself. The more you know about the way these big institutions and others do business, the more sense these concepts I am teaching will make, and the better the industry must become. You can change the world with your feet. Look, I am not saying that just because an investment group is fined that they are bad. With the vagueness and complexity of regulations today, it just takes a regulator having a bad day or perhaps wanting to retaliate or just shut someone up. I will talk about this in more detail later, but what I would be looking for in my investment firm, if I were you, is a pattern of noncompliance.

Noncompliance is a seemingly intentional and consistent skirting of the rules. I love good regulations and there are many, but we need to review and think about those that are either outdated or don't make any sense and remove or change them. Many can be simplified.

There are about 14,000 to 17,000 mutual funds from which an investor can choose. A mutual fund is a bundle of different corporate stocks and/or bonds. Let's stick with stock funds right now. How do you know if yours is any good? Guess what? Technology is here. The way I do it is I pull out my computer, ask the pertinent questions and give the program the correct criteria and voila, there's the answer. It's not rocket science for me. I have computer programs that compare all funds that a third-party rating system lists. You can give it multiple criteria and ask them to be listed in different orders, say maybe according to returns with a three-month, six-month or one to 10 year inception. So, if you are looking at growth funds, you can actually find out how yours stack up. However, I may not end up choosing the funds just because they're on the top of the performance list. There may be reasons why some of them are eliminated, and that's where experience, knowledge and industry connection come in.

But Stop! You've heard your broker say that past performance is not an indication of future returns. There is a regulation that requires them to say this to you. They write regulations to cover everything and I am sure there is a good reason for this one; however think for a minute. If you had two mechanics… Oh wait, I have two. My wife takes her car to the dealer. In fact she has a high dollar Cadillac. They keep the car for days, she has to always take it back and they find another part to change and they charge her an arm and a leg and they kill her with their price. I use Big Ed. I take my car there. He greets me with "Hi folks!" I am alone. I look behind me for someone else and I realize he is talking to me. I tell him my problem and he says he'll get to it as soon as he can. He calls me back two hours later. I pick it up. Pay him a price I am very pleased with and he says, "Good-bye folks." (Yes it's just me.) I go home never to return. Now who am I going back to? The same holds true with mutual fund managers. If I find a consistent performer on a 10-year basis and he outperforms other funds in good times and bad and he beats the index, where do you think I'll put my money? And I am looking at load adjusted returns. Now there is a little more that goes into the final decision, but doesn't this sound like a good way to start? Think about it. It's not rocket science. I monitor them for manager changes or changes in philosophy, and if they screw up, I fire them. I once had a 401k trustee for a large firm say, (proudly, I might add) "We don't chase returns."

I wanted to ask her, "So you are chasing losses?" Some broker with crap for funds must have said that to her as they stunk the place up. By the way, every fund we showed her, except one, outperformed theirs substantially and the one that didn't was one of the funds we use. I guess even a blind squirrel finds a nut every now and then. You just will not believe the differences. I can pretty well assure you of one thing: you don't have many, if any, good mutual funds in your portfolio. Prove me wrong!

I am often asked, "Why didn't my broker tell me about these other high-performing funds?"

To which I just reply, "Go ask her or him." (Mouse in the corner time.)

Normally what a transactional broker will say is that because these funds make more money they are higher risk. They will say that they are more "conservative" so that is why they are making less or loosing. Think about it. You were probably taken by this one because you remember someone saying "the higher the risk the higher the return." Then you misinterpreted what they said. They were actually trying to tell you that the riskier the investment the higher potential you have for greater returns. For instance if you have a wildcat oil well, it is usually a riskier play than if you are drilling a developmental well in a known field. The wildcat can open up a whole new field that you can participate in and your returns could be phenomenal but a run-of-the-mill production well will be average. I have seen brokers cover their own poor choices like this many times and you will fall for it. Think about it.

If you have two funds with equal risk (beta) on a 10-year basis and history has shown good times and bad, and one makes 10% on a load adjusted basis and one makes 20% which is the most risky? THE 10% ONE. Even when I tell this story and ask the question, people get the answer wrong the first time by force of habit. It means the 20% manager is superior to the other unless they had a lucky year or two. On a Morningstar report you can see each year. It's the manager's skill we rely on, folks. If they leave, we shall follow. Fees and commissions don't matter, I said, "load adjusted return."

Bonds

Remember I explained why the bond market isn't a good idea for you at this point in time? In Chapter 3, I pointed out that interest rates determine the yield on bonds. At a time when interest rates are low, such as now, you will lose money if interest rates increase to the tune of about $116 or more for every point they increase on a 20-year bond. In other words, who would want to buy your 4% bond when interest rates are at 8%, for example. They will buy it from you at a discount.

You must also consider round lots of bonds. A round lot is $100,000. This is how most bonds trade for the big boys. This market is eight times bigger than the stock market. You can buy smaller amounts, but you will pay a higher commission on the buy and the sell. In fact, it is very hard to sell small amounts of bonds because it may be hard to find a buyer. At the sale, the broker usually says something like, "If you hold these bonds to maturity you will get your money back." Let me ask you, does it sound like fun to be trapped with a 4% bond while everyone else is making much more? Bonds are a great invest-ment when interest rates are high. As interest rates decrease, the value of bonds increases. Sound better? You can buy an inflation protected security from the government and as long as the increase in interest rates is due to inflation you might be alright.

What if they rise for another reason? Let's say the Fed decides to raise them to do their market manipulations. The Fed tries to prevent inflation by raising interest rates to tighten the money supply while at the same time printing money that causes inflation. Go figure. I am sure they have a good reason. I am just too dumb to figure it out. I hate being logical, don't you? Besides, the government is such a well-run institution and they are so solvent. I dare say if a corporation was in the same financial shape as our government and made the same sort of wise business decisions, and had the same track record of success, we would all be standing in line to give them our money. NOT! We would be trying to put their CEO's in jail and the Noisemakers would be leading the charge. You folks please insert Larry the Cable Guy's apology here.

A Note About Corporations

A big problem with corporations today is the regulatory environment in which we live. As I've said before, competition always works unless government regulates the competition out or people cheat. In response to a regulation, some smart middle-management guy comes up with a scheme to circumvent the regulation and the dynamic changes. The scenario that is playing out among corporations today is that they are competing against the customer instead of for the customer. In the case of utilities, they must go to a governing body to raise prices. So they no longer care about you, they spend their time trying to lobby for higher prices and increases. This is similar to government unions. Who is going to say no to a pay raise? You? The government? Why would they? The government and the union are one and the same in the way they act.

On the other end of the spectrum, instead of making their products more beneficial and/or of better quality, they are competing to reduce costs; however, they can and will forget about the consumers.

Banks as Corporations

Another group on the corporate greed side is the banks who issue credit cards. They are gouging consumers with interest rates as high as 30% if they miss a payment and late fees as high as $150 instead of a reasonable rate like, say, $5.

The heads of many of today's corporations are not entrepreneurs, but managers. When faced with the difficulty of competing due to regulations, they exploit rather than compete and create. Currently, we have very little competition in the banking industry. For someone to start their own bank is next to impossible. The cost of a new charter is prohibitive. A true entrepreneur would ask, "Why don't I be fair to customers and let them pay the going rate plus 5% and a $10 late fee?" Instead of screwing the customer every time they turn around, the banks could decide not to raise a credit limit when it is maxed out. They could cut the consumer off until they pay it down. Banks would gain the reputation as having integrity, thereby attracting more consumers and the bank would keep consumers out of the dungeon and slavery of insurmountable debt. This makes sense for the consumer and for the bank, but a bank today won't do that. How did they pay all that TARP money back so quickly?

Some of the largest corporations in the United States are in bed with the government. They now have very little risk. They are being lured in to an unholy alliance with the government. Why would the CEOs be responsible if they know they will be bailed out by the treasury? The object of every corporate head now is to find a way to be too big to fail. The sky is the limit. The more these corporations go into hock and the more people they hire, the more likely they are to be bailed out by the government. It's like owing money to a bank. If you owe them little, they pounce on you. If you owe them a lot, they must work with you. The government is now using this same strategy with their unprecedented expansion. The more employees they have, the more votes and influence they buy. CEOs will have no incentive to make a profit. They should be held accountable the same way a small business-man is. If the small business guy does not make a profit, he doesn't get paid. A CEO should be the same. We must invest more of our money with people who NEED to make a profit. I will show you how to do it. This by itself will have the effect of making our large corporations profitable unless the government subsidizes them, which they will do if they get enough election donations.

Real Estate

When I mention real estate, many things will pop into a person's mind: houses, land, condos, commercial rent houses. We've all seen the infomercials that tell us all how to get rich if we follow the guru-of-the-day's advice. We can even buy it for no money down. Jeez, we'll believe about anything. Let's go play where the big boys play, shall we? Real estate investment used to be reserved for only the fabulously wealthy and the institutions and endowments. Times have changed and so has availability.

Entrepreneurs have figured out how to gather and raise money and allow the smaller investor to participate. This means YOU. Many are familiar with the term REITs (Real Estate Investment Trusts). You may have one, but probably not the kind I am going to tell you about. ,You may have heard about a mutual fund REIT. This which is different from a private, accredited or non-traded REIT.

A REIT is only a form of ownership, not an investment unto itself. A mutual fund REIT behaves like a stock and is liquid on a daily basis and its value fluctuates the same as a stock. It does not necessarily reflect the value of the underlying real estate. In other words, it has stock market type volatility.

One other type of REIT fund available for investors is a Regulation D non-traded REIT. You may have to be an accredited investor. This has income and net worth requirements. I am not going to go into the intricacies of such; you can discuss this and qualify through an advisor who deals in such things. We have been investing in these since 1995. We like the results and the diversification it offers.

These funds may buy, own, manage and rent back to the business or businesses that want to have money invested in the goods they sell or the services they offer. They want the money for new locations. In other words, IHOP sells pancakes, Walgreens sells general merchandise, Lowe's sells hardware, Best Buy sells electronics and HEB sells groceries. If they have money tied up in real estate, i.e., in the buildings that they use, then they don't have the cash to expand and build other locations. They would rather rent the property back from you. Funds now exist that allow you to own your own private portion of these huge real-estate rentals.

You can own specialty funds such as ones that only invest in commercial office space. Some only invest in entertainment-type spaces, some in retail, some in only shopping centers. Some funds invest only in real estate that profits during down times. The list of various types of Regulation D REITs goes on and on and on. In inflationary times real estate values may grow. In bad times the prices may fall. This up and down movement creates opportunity. I like down times for the opportunity to buy, but I like good times for liquidation opportunities. Simply put, it cycles. One needs to take advantage of this for appreciation purposes. This is what the REIT fund managers try to do. So the result may be that you receive the rents on your ownership and appreciation on liquidation.

To invest in this market takes experience and skill on the part of the advisor. They must have skills in due diligence, business, personal judgment, and be able to have connections in the industry. Normal wire house brokers are usually not allowed by the firm to invest in such things. A real estate market exists that is different from the stock real estate market, but they aren't going to tell you about it because they are not qualified to sell it.

This sort of investment property was owned by banks in the past, but it is now available for anybody. The big transactional brokerages have no incentive to tell you of these options because it falls outside of their expertise and their company's product marketing plan. They will sell you a stock mutual fund REIT and convince you that you are diversified into the real estate market. Beware of the broker who tells you, "It is just too risky." She may really be saying, "I don't have that." You may also invest in these same types of investments in a Limited Partnership or an LLC. Each form of ownership has different tax implications. Some funds also participate only in development. As a general rule, you might consider that the best opportunities for investment in existing real estate properties are during a bad economy and the best for development investment are in good economies, but the fund managers may do well in both cycles if they are talented.

Think about it. So you may like the idea of getting "mailbox" money at retirement with a possibility of appreciation from this type of investment.

Let's talk about some practical real estate applications and scenarios starting with you retired folks first. You know the ones who thought they could live happily ever after on their savings. How would you have in the past, or could you now, use real estate in your portfolio?

Number one: we must diversify within the real estate asset class. So we might look at an office REIT first. The first thought that goes through your mind because you have been listening to pundits is that we are about to have another crisis in this area. GOOD. A crisis is good. The prices are low and could go even lower. The ones who must restructure debt right now could be in trouble. We would look for an office REIT that is looking to help you ; not the current owner. So if you can buy at a discounted price, with good occupancy rates and cash flow to fund your retirement check, you can see why this might work. Would you agree?

How about retail real estate? Well, some might be good and others not. But if you target "down-time retail'" such as Big Lots, Dollar Tree, Lowe's, Wal-Mart, Sam's Club, CVS or Walgreens, Auto Zones, O'Reilly Auto Parts and grocery stores this could make sense for your monthly check. As with all real estate, there is a possibility of appreciation. This may be more evident in an inflationary cycle.

As for housing developments, there are not as many possibilities in the down times, but as a cycle recovers, there may be opportunities there for mostly appreciation.

When we look at entertainment-type properties, we can find possibilities if the properties are chosen correctly. No one sold their golf clubs or skis and snowboards. The opportunities in the down times would be more focused on local usage areas such as the areas where they will be patronized by locals instead of the "destination'" type resorts that depend on long distance travelers. As always, try to buy these things in funds from well-established companies that are licensed, registered and have been successfully in business for a while. Never buy from newbies. Let others lose their money.

Let's take a look at global real estate. Success in this type of investment depends on the advisor that you choose. You have to work with an experienced player that is familiar with the countries in which properties are located. If one can get comfortable with this, I think there will be some fantastic opportunities especially if you are working with an American company investing internationally.

It used to be true that most political risk was associated with foreign companies, but now the US is acting more like a Third World socialist style dictatorship than it ever has in its history, so diversifying offshore makes more sense than ever. Again, this type of investment shows good possibilities for income and appreciation.

If you are preparing for retirement and are within 10 years of that date, you may want to shift more assets out of the stock market to this area to lock in gain and possibly guard against the volatility and uncertainty in today's market.

If you are younger and accumulating, you can use the income from these assets to either be opportunistic and invest when the market appears to be low or dollar cost average as the cash comes in. You can't effectively take advantage of the market when it is down if you don't have anything generating cash. You can sell low to buy low in the market, and I don't think I would rely solely on rebalancing. You may just be fooling yourself.

Oil and Gas

Most people can relate to buying BP or Exxon stock, so they think they own oil and gas. In reality, they just own stock in a corporation that deals in the oil and gas industry. In the past, you may have made good money in your 401K that was loaded with oil and gas stocks, but when the Noisemakers demonized the oil and gas industries, stock went down. You must not fall prey to their anti-capitalist rhetoric.

What would they offer as an alternative? When they demonize you lose: Period.

If you went and bought non-stock oil and gas production assets and oil goes up, you're going to be happy instead of depressed as you pay more and more at the pump. If you buy a piece of a drilling operation, you are taking drilling risk with your money, but if you assess the risk you can participate as a partner in a program that has a number of wells in it and be in the oil industry and share in the profits of this commodity. You may get a tax write-off of the Intangible Drilling Costs (IDC'S) that reduce your taxes. In fact it may give 70% (up to 100%) of the amount invested as a write-off. The reason for this is that sometimes they miss the gas or oil. Dry hole! The income may also have tax advantages such as depletion allowances and passive activity losses that may be used to offset passive income from a real estate investments. Investment in oil and gas production or drilling is not correlated to the stock market and in an inflationary period the price may increase and therefore your income. Wouldn't you have been happy when everyone was paying $4 a gallon and $10 an MCF for natural gas if you owned it? In other words, when Exxon was demonized for making obscene profits, you would have been also. Own what you hate to buy. This is America, you can participate!

When Noisemakers are saying, "Stop giving (the rich) tax breaks and high energy prices," What they are really doing is demonizing entrepreneurs (small business and investors) and thereby taking money, opportunity and jobs away from you.

On the surface, Noisemakers say that their attempts to micromanage oil and gas production benefit the environment. A skilled manipulator will tell you the exact opposite of the truth and that is exactly what is happening in this case. Micromanaging oil and gas production doesn't benefit the environment, it only gives the government guys control and funds to buy more votes, which enables them to advance their purpose of validating their fantasies of their own self worth to cover up their past life's' pain and injury. These are the Noisemakers. They can do it no other way. They are not your friends or saviors. You must understand them and their self deceit. They are injured past the point of self redemption. In their minds they cannot lose. This is not because they believe they can't fail, but they must go to any length to preserve the imaginary self.

Controlling oil and gas production is not about the shortage of energy and dependence on foreign oil. It is about demonizing an industry, furthering belief in global warming and working to solidify central control. Ask yourself, "Where were politicians trained to understand the intricacies of the energy market, health care, global warming, investments, capitalism and on and on?" Are they really that much smarter than you?

Look at their backgrounds. Most are lawyers. Most have never been in any type of business or created a paycheck with their own dollars. Just where would they learn this stuff? They didn't. Why would you let them control anything in your world or the business world? Yes we need regulations, but many times the regulations are worse than the problem. This is not about regulation, it is about the people in charge of making regulations. If we were allowed to drill all of the available oil in the United States, we wouldn't ever have to buy petroleum from another country unless we wanted to, but regulations created by Noisemakers won't' let us drill in some of our most potentially lucrative locations. Noisemakers cannot stand being wrong. They will never change paths even if it means our destruction.

Managed Futures

Managed futures are a way of having predictable costs in the future. I say "managed" because you should not buy individual contracts yourself. Go to Vegas instead. Managed means there are funds that do this; some good and some bad. My father-in-law was an engineer and farmed corn and soybeans. He charted and graphed the grain market extensively for decades and never made a dime trading grain futures. When Southwest Airlines locked in oil and gas prices when they were low, they were able to keep costs low because they owned contracts in the future. They did not bet the farm. They did it with a portion of their assets. As an asset, managed futures allow you to take advantage of buying and selling at a lower or higher price in the future to make money by speculation or have predictable costs for a commodity. This is a very dangerous market for most, even for many of the professionals. This is a big boy game. It doesn't mean you can't participate, but you may not want to try this at home or you might get hurt. You need to hire the best. You need someone who makes this their life's work and has the most talent and a track record to prove it.

Remember Big Ed? Again, as with the rest of these investments, the big brokerage houses don't handle managed futures. You need to elevate your portfolio to match your success in life (or your desire to be) by going to an advisor that deals in such matters. Unless you understand the managed futures arena, you will lose. It can go both ways. For every winner, there is a loser. An example of this is when Tyson's Chicken bought a straddle in the cattle futures market. A straddle is both a winning and a losing bet for the price to go up or down, whichever direction the price went, they made money, but they also lost money. They then passed the winning side to Mrs. Clinton during her election campaign. If you did this you would most likely have been sitting next to Martha Stewart during her involuntary vacation in jail.

You can bet on the price of gold, silver, precious metals, world currencies, hog bellies, corn, soybeans and many others. One interesting strategy that may work during inflationary down market times is using gold as your currency. Some funds will convert your dollar into gold and if gold rises you make money with the gold. If they make money on the futures trades, you may also make money on that side. So if you think the US dollar value may decline and gold may go up, this is a good strategy. You can ride gold prices to the top and when the economy turns around the gold prices may decline and you convert your currency back to the dollar which will probably grow in value. You notice I always say "probably" because everything has a risk and unknown factors. Nothing is 100%. That is why you diversify into all eight asset classes and diversify within each asset class: short and sweet.

Equipment Leasing

Railroad cars, shipping containers, nuclear power plants, oil rigs, drilling ships, airplanes and cargo ships as well as oil tankers are owned by investors, not necessarily by the operating company. They lease them back from investors and pay a steady rent. There are different companies that trade, buy and sell leases. Banks are usually the institutions that originate a lease; they then at some point will sell the lease for various reasons. The expensive part of the leasing process is the origination. I usually will stay away from companies that will originate their own leases, I prefer they cook for a while. They seem more stable after they have been allowed to, shall we say, sauté. Leasing funds may then purchase various types and diversify within their portfolio. Their objective is to give investors a nice check each month or quarter and return principal at the end of a certain time period. They may be planning to sell the leases themselves or the underlying assets in the lease.

This is the tricky part: the liquidation. They should be loading their fund with the end game (liquidation) in mind. If they must sell assets, they must have factored in any depreciation in value and have made up the decline somewhere else. If not, or if there is a problem, the investor may not get their principal back. Sometimes they are paying out both principal and interest and at the end of the program the last payment is the last payment. No Mas! If you planned this then OK, but it better not be a surprise to you, huh! This is similar to the Ginny Mae-type funds that paid out principal and interest and someone's grandmother was really happy with her large monthly payment, but did not understand that they were also paying back her principal a little at a time and she was spending it all. This could be OK if the principal portion was set aside or they were letting something else grow to replace this principal. It is also great for accumulators.

They can dollar cost average out of the equipment leasing fund into the stock market on a monthly basis and thereby combine their investments into a potentially profitable or risk lowering strategy.

Some funds will allow you to purchase an equity side or a note side. In this scenario, if the fund has any problems, the note holders will receive their money and perhaps a preferred return before the equity partners receive theirs. If a profit exists on the liquidation of the fund, the note holders will not participate, only the equity holders share in any profits. There would, therefore, be more risk to the equity holder, but more potential for appreciation. At the time of the writing of this book, interest rates are historically low for retired investor income. I have seen programs that are paying 8-9% returns without distributing principal. I guess I don't have to explain how this might work for you since you are beginning to develop a keen eye for the obvious.

Equipment leasing is part of a good investment portfolio that is not correlated to stock market, bond market, oil and gas, futures options and so on. This is the trick! If I could predict the future, I could be King of the World, but I can't. So I am saying that if we have eight different non-correlated or loosely correlated classes, it is only logical that we may lower our risk and have something in our portfolio that is making money.

As interest rates tanked, and we had our severe recession, the equipment leasing stuff just kept plodding along, but at some point in time, it may have problems and we hope something else takes its place. When bad things happen in one area, then opportunities may be created elsewhere.

When real estate values went down, many had their dividend payments decrease as the mangers re-rented space and had to spend money for new tenant move-ins and improvements. You could hedge this by buying into distressed real estate while your equipment leasing kept paying right along and if you were smart you sold stocks when things were good and bought gold as the market was having problems, and so on. See how it is starting to come together? The hope is that something is always making you money, since there is no one form of investment that is going to make money all of the time.

Notes and Credit

Corporations and businesses are having a hard time finding money for expansion and operations. In normal times they have access to bank loans, but today the banks are tight with money because they are trying to maintain their solvency and their loan-to-asset ratio. They may be concerned that many real estate assets will be devalued and before they know it, the FDIC has an auditor at the door to shut them down.

The Noisemakers have decided to demonize and socialize the banking industry. Some were even forced to take TARP money when they didn't need it. There is a pay CZAR running around telling folks how much they get to make. Slow down for a minute and think about what that means. The government caused the banking problem and then took the opportunity to more or less "nationalize" by controlling and regulating the banking industry. They are in the process at this time of rewriting the banking laws to inhibit the banking industry from taking too much "risk." This is risk that the same government forced them to take in the Fair Housing Act.

We need to reclaim our government if we are to survive. I mean we need to actively participate as citizens in our own government. We seem content to calmly discuss the issues as they keep instituting their insanity. As reasonable people, that is what we do, however they are demonizing any opposition by saying the opposition is instigating violence and they feel frightened. These are typical Noisemaker tactics. They are not reasonable people and yet, they depend on you being lulled into a sense of safety; which you will be.

If you use the very same tactics they use, and you question the government as I have here, you will be attacked by the media as being a violent right-wing extremist, a racist and a danger to society. You may even be called a "tea bagger." Isn't the President supposed to be a unifier?

You can revolt at the ballot box. They will try to influence the ballot though, don't think they won't. Why do you suppose they moved the census into the executive branch? Why were members of the Black Panthers standing at polling places with clubs and were not prosecuted? What do you think ACORN and its hundreds of affiliates are all about? Remember hanging chads?

Back to notes and credit. If the banks won't loan money to our businesses, someone will. Why not you? The entrepreneurs of America are putting together private note funds to take up the slack. These folks have various types of innovative funds that raise money from you and you become the "bank."

They may loan money as a note and it might even be secured by a first lien on assets to assure, but not guarantee, that you have a level of safety. Some may have a "senior" status which means you must receive your money before any stock or bond holders receive theirs. Because this is not traditional bank money, the lender (you) may command a higher interest rate return than a bank.

Private Equity

Private equity is like the stock market, in the fact that they are ownership dollars, but it is riskier because there are fewer if any registration requirements, and therefore, a very different kind of risk for the uninformed. Anyone can ask you for money. Here is where people can do about anything. It is also a big boys' game also. Many large family offices participate in this market. Some of these folks look for small or middle-sized companies that either need an infusion of cash or talent, but may not want to go the route of going public. Some are very specific on what they will buy or invest. They may be opportunists that will develop a specific real estate deal such as a nursing home development. They may put it in a fund or just do a one-time thing. They may get all their money from one source or a variety of sources. The sky is truly the limit here. Entrepreneurs may hit a ceiling of competence or lack the cash to expand. Private equity provides their services to these folks.

Many things go on here. There are private equity firms that provide angel money for business starts. If they think you have a good idea, they will help you develop it. They may want a substantial piece of the ownership of the company for doing so. If you are in the fund they are using for financing these startups, this may present a profitable opportunity, but as you know, many businesses fail at startup. However, if the private equity group is talented, they may be able to mitigate some of the risk with management assistance (they may have their own people on the board) and control. Private equity funds may raise money for development also. Many are developing senior living facilities. These facilities are much needed and may be quite profitable.

Tax Credits

Tax credits were initiated by the federal government to provide incentives to contractors and developers to build low-income housing. Before tax credits, there was not much interest in building this type of facility for obvious reasons. No profit! The federal government would allocate certain credits to the states and the states would issue them to developers. Many times they would dole out 150% credit to be given out on an annual rate of 15% for ten years. The properties had to be held for 15 years and then the properties could be sold and the investor might receive a partial or total return of principal. A tax credit is different from a deduction because it is a dollar-for-dollar reduction of taxes.

I don't recommend tax credits as an investment at this time, though they could come back. The non-profits have gotten into this industry and commercial developers have stopped building these facilities with private investors. This kind of housing used to be for people who were at 60% of the median income of their particular area so many times you could attract high quality tenants, such as teachers or firemen. In other words, we the taxpayers are subsidizing the tenants. You can also get a tax credit for historic rehabilitation. So if you can purchase a house and have it qualify as a historic structure, you may be able to get a tax credit to do so.

Geopolitical Influences

Many people speculate on whether or not they should put their money into developing country infrastructures or industries. Developing countries are growing because they can produce what we produce more cheaply. We can still out-produce these countries, but the more we are taxed and regulated, the more American companies are moving overseas. The more we tax ourselves, the less competitive we will be and the more jobs we will lose. The thing that keeps us ahead in spite of our over-regulated government is that these developing countries are so corrupt. We tax; they just steal from their people. You can't rule over people. Citizens must have the freedom and natural spirit to communicate and create. Evil only exists in the absence of good. As long as we the citizens of the United States of America stand up and participate in our government, insuring a free capitalist economy, then we are the country to invest in.

Corporate Noisemakers ally themselves with the government, using the government to increase their profit. When there is understanding among the people of their relationship to capitalism, that can't happen. Large brokerage houses and bankers have lost the entrepreneurial spirit and become Noisemakers. They have become engrossed in regulations and what they can get away with. Today's marketplace battle is not customer-centered; rather, it is a contest to see who can get away with what. As morals decline, so do returns on investments.

Grow your wealth, and, in the process, grow your participation in the free market economy. Take charge of how you think and act. Stand independently of the stock market, the investment industry and even your own fear. You are in charge. Make decisions about your money that create more money.

You have the power: use it!

Noise Level Check: Chapter 5

1. If you had $10M right now, what would you do with it? Make a list, showing the long and short-term gain of each form of investment. Note the kind of research and professional support you will need and include that cost.

2. What happens, in your opinion, to the economy when the really wealthy people lose money?

3. How are the really wealthy people connected to the middle class?

4. Can the middle-class and the poor trust the wealthy people to use their money wisely, or is the government right in trying to address humanitarian concerns via tax dollars?

5. Do you think you can make a difference by thinking and talking about politics and economics with the people that you know, or is this a way of deluding yourself that your opinion matters in an oversized machine?

6. Do you think you can make a difference by writing and calling your elected representatives?

7. If you were starting a new country today, how would you set up the economy and the government? Be specific about the powers of the government and the way that the taxes and regulations would interact with businesses.

Do you have additional thoughts you would like to share with me about this chapter, or questions? I want to know what you think! Email me at steve@thenoisemakersbook.com

A popular Government, without popular information,

or the means of acquiring it,

is but a Prologue to a Farce or a Tragedy;

or, perhaps both. Knowledge will forever govern ignorance:

And a people who mean to be their own Governors,

must arm themselves with the power which knowledge gives.

~ James Madison,

letter to W.T. Barry, August 4, 1822

The Econo-penny

in

Your Pocket

Individuals with money to invest often consider purchasing rental properties, oil wells, livestock, land, boats, airplanes, gold, businesses, jewelry or cars. They reason they do this is that these things have value, can hopefully be resold at higher prices and can maintain assets separate from the stock market. They are scared to death of the conventional methods because they keep losing money doing what the investment companies tell them to do. They have a keen eye for the obvious—they keep losing money on a regular basis while being told everything will be fine if they just hold on for a little longer. Do you recognize this type of "long-term investor?" Millions of individuals making spending mistakes adds up to one big bad economy.

If you keep following this dumb notion, your financial success will be short-lived. I suggest to you that the only thing that should relate to you being a long-term investor is that you have a long life. I would argue that, I understand your thinking, but generally speaking, these sorts of investments expose you to loss and are not worth the risk. What sorts of investments am I talking about? Here are a few.

Residential Real Estate

People make large purchases oftentimes with these rationalizations: "I can't do any worse than what the stock market is doing to me." That's because you relied on the wrong people at the wrong time, doing the wrong things. You misinterpreted being a long-term investor. Yes, you are long-term because you have a whole life to invest, but you thought that meant you never move anything, you ride out the ups and downs of the market all the time and you thought when stocks go up, bonds go down and so on and so on and so on. How hum drum! I get depressed just saying this junk. You relied on the two-product wonders, selling things for every reason except YOU making money and the "advisors" all look the same, sound the same and you thought there was no other choice. I've taught you how to avoid this. Wake up.

Some people go out and want to buy and manage rental properties. Whenever one of my clients asks me about rental properties as an investment, I mention, trash, tenants and toilets. Most renters don't care about the property, so you will have to repair and repaint each time you acquire new tenants. In addition, you have to fix every major and minor repair associated with those houses. Finally, if you end up with a bad tenant, evicting them is a long and expensive process. In some states, a landlord cannot enter their own rental property without the tenant's permission.

As for resale value on rental properties, you have to buy at the right price. To break even, consider property taxes and expenses. Is it a new or an old structure? How much can you rent it for on a consistent basis? What are the payments? For example, combine $5k in payments with insurance and property taxes (and you count on them to go up). This brings your total outflow to $9k a month. You would have to charge people to pay their rent plus your profit.

When it comes to rental property, you have to find a property where the costs plus the rental income means that it will at least pay for itself, if not generate a profit. Then, it must appreciate in value for resale. Finally, a positive outcome depends on finding the right tenant. Does this make sense as a business? It might if you dedicate all of your time and you are a very good repair person who has the temperament to put up with about anything. Most never make a dime, but that late night infomercial sure looked easy. If it were so good, why didn't that guy keep his mouth shut? He gave away his strategy. Do you think he did that out of the kindness of his heart, or could it be he found an easier way???? HMM YA THINK?

As I suggested earlier, partner with an advisor who is talented at picking real estate sponsors who align their interest with you and sit back and collect the "mailbox" money and probably even experience some appreciation. Many of these folks subordinate their profits to you making x% per year on a cumulative basis.

California is a good example of individual property management risk. Because of market fluctuations, many people do not end up making a profit. People who paid $1M for a house a short time ago are now getting $400K. If you have a duplex, you can depreciate the value if it's a business. Have you heard of the capital gains tax and recapture? During the sale you can end up paying 25% to 30% of your gain in taxes. If you paid $1M for the property 10 years ago and now it's worth $600K, and you depreciated out the property you could sell it for $600K and still have to pay a 15% capital gains tax or 25% recapture even though you lost money on the deal. Look for capital gains tax to go up to at least 28%.

Would you rather be renting to Lowe's, HEB, Auto Zone, the US Government, FedEx, Best Buy, Wal-Mart, Dollar Tree, Walgreens and CVS? Compare these triple A rated companies (who are responsible for all maintenance) to ordinary people. Let's see, why are they renting? The risk is far less. Not that there is no risk, but think about it. Sounds good in a conversation with your buds at the club, or wherever you are.

If you love rental properties, make your investments on the commercial real estate side. If you already own investment residential real estate, know that eventually, when you decide that you have had enough trash, tenants and toilets, you will be able to do a 1031 like kind exchange.

When I can't sleep at night, I turn on the TV at 3 AM. I'll watch an infomercial on how to make $1M on real estate. The guy paints a glowing picture: buy foreclosed houses, repaint them and resell them. This is not for most people. If it worked really, really well, I would have heard about it.

Cattle and Other Livestock

Many people in Texas raise cattle. They can get an agricultural tax exemption and they love it. In fact, some love it so much, they raise cattle until they go broke. The price of hay and feed, land upkeep, siring, transport, herding and outbuildings and vet bills far exceeds the fluctuating profit on a steer or cow for some. So if you love it, good luck. Just don't put all your eggs in one basket. I wonder how much the new health care folks will like the red meat thaing?

Boats and Airplanes

I personally own two airplanes and a large fishing boat. Everything that I do in my life has some sort of financial meaning to it. I can charter my fishing boat and I can use it to make money on tournament fishing kind of like the NASCAR guys and gals. When I chartered the boat, I made money getting acquainted with the type of people I needed to be acquainted with while fishing. As a financial advisor you can't walk up and down the dock and say, "I'm a financial coach, why don't you give me all of your money?" My financial business sponsors my fishing boat in tournaments and people see our Web page, and I develop relationships with people to create win-win situations. If I run the boat in a tournament, my boat business makes money and then I can possibly meet potential investors in an environment where they can get to know me and learn what type of character I have. People do business with those whom they know and trust. I had a Coast Guard license and I am a fairly (rare and unintended and disingenuous modesty....confident, yes that's the ticket; confident) good competitive fisherman. I've won some tournaments and winning has had many positive results other than the prize money. I feel like I can win them all in the same way a golfer or any other competitive person thinks he or she can win every one they enter. I have employed many in these endeavors to maintain and fish on the boat.

I'm an entrepreneurial unit. So are you. As entrepreneurial units, we must try to be profitable in everything we do. Profit isn't always seen as directly getting an income from what you are doing, but that is my motive in my life. Everyone has a score card and when I make money it means I am serving a lot of people well. I try to serve as many people in as many ways as I can imagine to improve their lives, and as a result it improves mine and my family's. There is nothing wrong with turning something you love into a profit center. It is not a requirement that you are miserable in a job and you can't wait until you are 65 and retire. I fell like I have been retired for most of my life and my endeavors are the permanent vacation that pays an income. It wasn't like falling off a log though. I had to take tremendous risk and devote many hours to creation, experimentation, failure and pressure to finally get to where I am today. I realize that I could lose it all tomorrow because of the political risk we all now experience. I started fishing with a 14-foot John boat and now have a 54-foot fishing boat. I think you can do it also if we all remember to keep the American spirit alive by allowing entrepreneurs the financial freedom to develop. The Noisemakers are taking the next generations' opportunities away. They are absolutely ruining the country by destroying the human spirit. They are elevating themselves by destroying others.

My plane use is 99.999% business. I can meet my clients where they live and give the personal touch. I have offices in several cities. My clients like to see that I am successful. It makes sense to have these things for business travel and for the identification purposes. I got sick to my stomach when I saw those corporate executives apologizing for flying over on the companies jets. Time is money for the stockholders. The Noisemaker news media jumped right on board to demonize these people and as a result everyone was afraid to fly corporate jets for a while and therefore the industry was hurt. Especially the so called "little guy."

When you are asking yourself, "Should I buy this boat?" or "Should I buy this plane?" evaluate how many different ways you can use that boat or plane or fancy car to help you create more opportunities to serve and therefore make more money for yourself and therefore others.

The better you do, the more money and jobs you create for others. The government actually makes more money also because they can collect more taxes. If they don't know this, they shouldn't be in office. Ooops, that eliminates about 70% of them. If you can't find solid financial reasons to make the purchase, walk away! Always get a deal. You will find yourself wearing waders and cleaning the sides of a money-sucking purchase or shelling out hanger fees or practically begging for buyers to take your aging sports car off your hands.

Land as an Investment or Income.

Many people buy or inherit land. I've heard the saying "they don't make any more land." They seem to say it is valuable and is an asset that can't go away. The Noisemakers know no bounds, but they are not yet ready to tackle this one. Your 401ks and IRAs first. They have talked about it. Look at all the land the government owns now. They lease it to folks for oil, ranching and other endeavors. It is income for them. Most of some western states are owned by the federal government. My point here is not to discourage you from buying land, but to warn you of what can happen if we continue on our current path. I've also noticed that the people who say they, "don't make any more land" deal never sell their land. Many times it is lazy land. Iowa farmers beat their brains out to barely make it and depend on government subsidies to help make a profit. This is how the Noisemakers got to own the farm vote. Noisemakers are incrementalists in the same vein as regulators; every one of them has to make his name by grabbing more for himself by taking it from you while trying to fool you into thinking they are Robin Hood. The difference is Robin Hood stole from an oppressive government and gave it to the people. Our Robin Hood is stealing from the people and giving to themselves. I guess we should call them Robbing Hoods. They have no intention of helping the poor; they are buying the votes by creating dependency of the people. They want you to look at them for the answers and the money. Can't work, never has, never will.

I get asked a lot (being in Texas), "Should I sell the ranch?" In Texas many people are land rich and/or cash poor. If it's not doing anything for you business-wise, it won't give you a monetary return. If it don't make no monies, it is an albatross that drain your chi-ching. When you own land, you have to have buyers and pay taxes. In the case of land that holds oil leases, that could be a good investment. Is there any oil? Before you make a land purchase, you need to find a way to make it an active asset. Assets can't be lazy.

The decision to buy or sell a large asset needs to be made by answering this question: What do you want to achieve? Most people do not want to achieve money loss, but they mistakenly think that their purchase will become more valuable over time. Some people will do the craziest things without a hope to make money on it. I listen to my clients' ideas regarding a possible purchase and I repeat back to them what they said. When I'm sitting across the table from someone and I ask them, "What do you want to achieve?" They can become very quiet, realizing that either they have no goal in mind or that this purchase will not help them achieve the goal they do have in mind. Think it through. Dreaming is great, maybe you are another Bill Gates or maybe ....?

Gold

When it comes to buying gold, consider what kind of gold you might buy. Are you considering purchasing gold coins? Gold coins normally will cost you more than raw gold. Then, what are you going to do with the gold? What if the price of gold goes way up? Are you going to sell it when it's high? It may get higher. Then again, you may want to sell it when times are hard and you need the money, but then who would want to buy it? When you buy something concrete that fluctuates in price, it creates nothing. When you buy a bar of gold, did you create jobs? I have seen lately the pro-business conservatives hawking gold in their commercials. They are taking money out of the economy thinking they are preserving something. Gold creates nothing but gives the false sense of security that you will be fine if the system collapses. Dream on. Who wants your gold when there is no system? I would rather have a bunch of chickens. I can't eat your gold and you don't have enough gold for me to give you a chicken. Remember, when you invest in something that creates jobs, you actually ensure that you'll have a job. Your job depends on the capitalist system, so invest in creating money and creating jobs.

Jewelry

I know people who buy bracelets, rings and necklaces that are worth hundreds of thousands, even millions of dollars because it is an investment. They will get half of what they've paid for that jewelry—if they're lucky. To check on the true asset value of your jewelry, take it to a jeweler or put an ad in the paper listing the appraisal value. Tell people you want to sell for the appraised value. Find out if the jewelry will sell for even 50% or 60% of its appraised value when times are good.

If you want to see if what you're doing is working, evaluate it. Pretend that you have to liquidate and observe the marketplace results.

Oil Wells

People were upset when they had to pay $6 for gas a while back, but my investors were happy because they own gas and gas production. It is a good investment strategy to own whatever you hate to buy.

In Texas, we get a lot of propositions for investing in oil wells. Besides whether or not the well has oil, there are other aspects to consider. The problem with investing in oil wells is that it can be very risky because there are so many different kinds of programs. The typical person calling you to get you to invest in an oil well has a program to offer that is not investor-friendly. The average program takes you to the cleaners on fees.

You can put together your own program if you know what you are doing. So, like investing in futures, if you want to invest in oil, get hold of a seasoned oil well investment advisor first. It is not an investment for the novice. The problem is that there aren't many good choices here, but there are some. Someone has to really know their stuff.

One way you can make money on an oil well is by drilling a number of offset wells on the East Coast. There are companies out there that raise money for this sort of thing. Many times they will hit 90 or more out of 100 of them and they will produce a little for a long time, providing nice tax write-offs. Because drilling risk is minimized, this is good for some. The program gives a reasonable income, but it is not a barn buster. Different areas in the country offer different risks and, therefore, different returns. In this industry there is a defiant relationship between risk and return. New areas offer the potential for great returns at a high risk, but if you can get in there first, many times you have rights to develop the area. There are new discoveries offshore in the Gulf as well as the mainland and the East Coast, the Rocky Mountains, the Dakotas, Texas, Alaska. We have large numbers of areas yet to be tapped, but it does not fit the Noisemaker agenda so the political risk is ominous. You must not buy into their "environmental concerns." They do not exist to the extent they would have you believe.

When you go with oil, you never want to invest in just one well. Invest in a number of wells and make sure that the oil company doesn't cherry pick the best wells for themselves.

There are exploration wells, wildcatting wells or buying oil out of wells that are already producing. The oil well industry is a big industry and it is not as simple as it seems. I am not talking about stocks. You can buy oil and gas company stocks, but I am talking direct ownership. It's like you're doing the business except you are hiring experts to work for you. You must know who the best people are to hire.

Again, while investing in oil wells can be productive, you must have an experienced advisor. Do not trust just any company. You are making a judgment call.

Stay in the United States or Leave the United States?

When deciding where to live and do business, one way you can vote is with your feet. I left Iowa because there was no economic growth in the state at that time. Our town went up substantially in population while I was growing up. Housing, construction, new industries; you name it we were getting it. We had a major railroad as well as the Mississippi River for transportation. It was a safe little town where you never had to lock your door at home and you could leave the keys in your car. It grew explosively as a lot of businesses moved in during the 50's, 60's, 70's. Then somewhere along in there, Iowa raised its state income tax to almost 10%. Guess what? Companies shut down and moved out. The town I lived in started shrinking. College grads moved out. People who had money moved out, so people who remained had to pay more of a tax burden and these were the people who in many cases could least afford it. Do you think the government started spending less money? No! If you don't believe in this death spiral, just look at California and Michigan right now. This ain't rocket science. It's Noisemaker science. This is not a spiritual concept. You can see it, feel it and experience it: you just have not contemplated it. You just can't understand why anyone would want to do it, especially since they sound so sincere when they say they are not doing this. They can't help it. It is what they do. There have been numerous past and present figures that do these things and they are smart enough to only take it far enough to stop and let you "normalize" the behavior and then move on. They will go as far as they can each time and they never give up. They call it *compromise*, but only compromise in their direction and ask for a lot and take what ever you will give them and will get the rest later.

A lot of people are moving out of the United States to retire because they can live on their social security check in Costa Rica. Many are forced to move because it's cheaper and some just choose to. (If you are planning on relying on social security for your retirement, remember: social security is a ponzi scheme. It is broke. The money a retiree makes now is not the money they invested, but your money. When you are ready to retire, where will your money be?) The Noisemakers will be after your 401k soon. They must. Foreign countries will refuse to loan us money soon or when they do it will be at such high rates our ridiculous deficit will be even higher. They will develop an annuity program. They will say they must because you cannot trust the capitalist stock market. You know….because it keeps losing all your money and all these CEO crooks are stealing it all. It is just too risky for you, so we are here to solve this crisis (which they so successfully caused themselves) and we will give you a guaranteed annuity. We will take your 401k and IRA money and put it into this safe annuity and you can take an income at retirement. Guess what! The money will be invested in…..you guessed it; government bonds. Guaranteed by the federal government. Then they will have no deficit and even a balance budget, but they can't help themselves and they will not reduce spending, but increase it to buy more votes and will borrow all the money out and replace it with an IOU as they did with social security and we, we'll be bent over again. So you will be paying your own interest on something that won't exist.

Many wealthy people have tried to move money to Switzerland and other places. Recently the United States government has convinced the Swiss government and others to disclose US citizen bank accounts. The US government is trying to slow citizen exodus because they know that there is less taxation in other places in the world. They have closed our borders financially for those who wish to leave, but leave them open to those who may drag us down. If America were a great country as we used to be, everyone would be trying to bring their money here, not get it out. The Europeans were, but now are screeching to a halt. We must make America a place where everyone is trying to bring their money as it once was, not a place where those with nothing come to drain services in trade for their self-serving vote. At some point in time if this continues, they will have to close the borders to people departing.

Recently, I rode a plane out of the country and was asked by an official at the door of the plane, "How much money do you have with you?" I said it was none of his business. He said he needed to know.

I said, "No you don't. I will fill out my required form." The questionnaire asks me: "Do you have more than $10K or more than $50K in cash or securities?" The United States government will be forced to close the door to immigration, so if you're going to go, you better go - soon. The Noisemakers won't allow a massive outflow of rich people from its borders. For a while, they may let the people go, but not the money.

We need to find reasons for these rich people to stay. Everything will work right if you create the opportunities that our system demands and that we allow.

The way you do that is with your vote. Those people in the middle-class thinking that the Noisemakers are going to help them by taxing the rich don't realize that these increased taxes on the rich will have the opposite effect. First of all, they will discourage the creation of more money and more jobs. Secondly, greater taxing of the rich will prompt an outflow of wealth from this country to countries with less taxation. Wake up; you are losing your jobs to companies moving out now. If poor Mexicans can cross the border and not get caught, don't you think rich people will figure out a way to leave? If the rich person will make money reinvesting in our economy, he will. If he can't, he won't. It's our responsibility as citizens of the United States of America to understand our relationship to the capitalist economy and then to vote to ensure the health and long life of that economy. Countries are giving incentives for us to come to them. Americans don't want to leave, but you cannot believe the revolution of the rich or others to being ruled over or vilified. They will go where they are appreciated. Oprah built her school in Africa even as American blacks suffer in our inner-city schools.

Keep your wits about you as an investor and as a citizen; don't be a Bambi. Be a reasonable man or woman living in the greatest country on Earth. Listen, analyze and act.

1.   Now that you know more about rental real estate, would you consider investing in it? If not, what would you chose instead?

2.   Do you think it's economically wise to continue living in the United States at this time? Why or why not?

3.   If you had an extra $300,000 on hand, what would you do with it?

4.   What is your opinion of gold as an investment?

5.   Why do you own the concrete assets that you have? What changes would you like to make?

6.   How can you alter your portfolio to create more stability and long-term gain?

7.   What is your top priority when it comes to how you live your life? How is this reflected in your monetary investments?

Do you have additional thoughts you would like to share with me about this chapter, or questions? I want to know what you think! Email me at steve@thenoisemakersbook.com.

A fondness for power is implanted

in most men, and it is natural to abuse it, when acquired.

~ Alexander Hamilton,

The Farmer Refuted, February 23, 1775

We

Star Spangled

Flashlights

In these dark days of economic depression, the greatest light we have is our choice to participate in our government as citizens. Turn on CNN or FOX and you will hear a political pundit talking about how, with years of plenty, Americans stopped paying a lot of attention to their own government. They mention the words, "laziness" and "focus." The truth is that if you want to avoid being shot and stuffed...again, then you've got to pay attention. You got complacent and you trusted your elected representatives, regulators and CEO' to do the right thing. If you went walking in the woods in Maine during hunting season, wouldn't you wear bright orange and sing *She'll Be Comin' Around the Mountain* in a loud voice? Well, now here you are, walking through the woods of economic meltdown, political partisanship and civil unrest and protest. What are you going to do? Here's what I suggest: pull out your star spangled flashlight.

Get out of the linear thinking process. Stop accepting what you are taught. Now is the time to trust and develop your intuitive judgments. Quit being co-dependent[1]. To be successful in dealing with other people and avoid getting the wool pulled over your eyes, you've got to pull out your multi-point reasoning and scope. Herds follow nothing except a fearful instinct. Get out of the herd mentality. Stop looking for an "expert" or an "authority" to tell you what to do. Quit being emotionally locked up and therefore blind to your own process of critical thinking. Stop passing around stupid emails designed to marginalize those passing them around. Remember these people you are trusting? Well believe me, they don't know you and those that do may not be your friend! They appear to be your friend and say all the right stuff and make you feel good about them, but so did all the despots of history. You, you the citizen of the United States, with all of the information in the world at your fingertips and all of the civil rights to use that information, you must inform yourself and you must make up your mind and you must act. You must think it through.

Here is the way that I think when I watch "experts" talking on TV. I think, "Economic and environmental people are saying that the US can be a leader in that area for the rest of the world. What are they talking about? We are already ahead of every other country in the world environmentally anyway." Consider how expensive it would be for us to invest even more money into "going green." To decrease carbon emissions in the US by 1% would cost trillions. Hmm, come to think about it, you are a carbon unit and you expel carbon dioxide. So much money already goes toward developing renewable energy. If you can do it, you would be extraordinarily rich. So, if we were to decrease from, say 1000 parts per billion to 900 parts per billion how much difference would it make to the environment? Not much, but it would make a difference to our struggling economy. The United States can't be a leader in anything if our economy is going broke. Certainly, we don't want China and India to control us, but a better way of preventing that is to focus on our debt rather than out-racing them in terms of alternative energy. They are not even trying. These are the kinds of thoughts that I have as I listen to experts tell me what to think. What kind of nonlinear thoughts do you have?

You know, many educated folks all learned the same things. I thank God every day I did not go to college. I feel I have an unfair advantage. I think things they do not. My thought processes are different because I was privileged enough to learn myself. It helped that I read the World Book Encyclopedia at around eight years old and I did study things. I just had a different process. School bored me to death. I didn't study under somebody, I studied under everybody. I have nothing against college. I would have learned very little. I have been very profitable unconventionally. I don't criticize you for your path, I wish you well and know people can be successful either way. Read *The Outliers* by Malcolm Gladwell

I'm a fisherman and I know that if you build oil wells in the sea the well produces structures in which fish live and breed. We've had oil wells in Texas for many years and haven't had leaks. Unfortunately Louisiana had a big one. Much of the oil seems to have....disappeared. Hmm. It is a terrible thing that could have been handled much better by all for the citizens of the Bayou State. In California, the people don't want offshore drilling, but they do want more fish in their environment. You know, oil is a natural substance. It came from plant and animal life. Our garbage dumps will be very profitable to someone in a few hundred million years. The earth has been around for billions of years and has almost completely destroyed itself about four times. We exaggerate our own present-day importance just as man has always done. You would think we have been here forever. Where did that first living cell come from? Where was the Big Bang and what exploded? People don't think through their opinions. They act according to emotion and to the herd around them. I love engaging people who are stuck in a thinking habit and helping them to gently begin to consider ideas outside of their comfort zone. I don't care what method and mode that I use. The more people that read this book and decide they need to either write to me or talk about their ideas to someone else the better. Democracy isn't about agreement among all; it's about engagement among all!

Speaking of engagement, have you noticed already how the Noisemakers are trying to destroy the Tea Party by pitting it against itself? Power and greed will always try to co-opt original ideas, enthusiasm and true leadership. A true leader will ask more questions than they give answers. Their goal is to model for you the way to figure out your own government, not to figure it out for you. Independent thinking should control what goes on in this country.

Each family is an entrepreneurial unit. Each person in each family needs to look at themselves as they are an entrepreneurial unit. They are a cohesive unit that thinks and educates each other. Some members will be interested in education, others in finance, politics or energy. The idea is to bring everyone on board and have full participation in the discussions. Ask kids what they learned because when they come out of school they don't really know how things work. They have an education, but they don't know how to think. A good example of this is Barack Obama. Some people are surprised that the President doesn't know how to create jobs and get the economy moving. He was a lawyer and community organizer. He organized people but he never ran a business. He has no experience dealing with the regulations and other issues surrounding jobs. As a career politician, Obama is used to people giving him money because he asks for it. Where in that process would he have learned how the economy works and how businesses and jobs are created? Some think he does, and is destroying things on purpose. Perhaps he does, but if he truly understood, he would embrace capitalism because he would understand it creates more for the government.

In the investment classes that I teach at night, I have students who are brilliantly educated and who have never been down the entrepreneurial road. They don't know how to handle the creation of money or their investments. They do not know the correlation between investment, employment and self-created money and an ever-expanding economy that makes their 401k grow. They don't understand that a government job is a drain and an expense that steals from their future. Look at your life and family as an entrepreneurial unit and ask, "Why?"

For example, you may have a family member who thinks liberals are crazy and are stupid. Without taking their opinions personally, ask them, "What do you think the liberal frame-of-reference is and why do they do what they do and what are they saying?" You may discover that someone in your family thinks along the same lines, or that you do. At times, I throw up my hands until I remember the argument they are engaged in is not about logic. They have a different thing going on in their mind about trust and they can't tell you why, but they just don't feel right about something. They may have been injured by an employer, so all business owners are cruel and only in it for themselves.

Employers have been injured by employees and react by abusing or not trusting people. It is a difficult life. We are all human. But in America, we are all Americans and we have a constitution which we are all sworn to uphold. We have as a people the Ten Commandments[2], and even if you do not believe in God or are not a Christian or a Jew, I don't think you can find fault in those commandments. Let's use the rules.

Practice nonlinear thinking and open-minded questioning with your neighbors and at church. They say you should never discuss religion and politics, but you should engage with a method of understanding in a nonemotional way. For liberals, you may want to engage a conservative and just think through it. Say to yourself, "Maybe there's a way I can help them understand where I'm coming from and maybe there's a path that will make things better for both of us. Let's think this through together so we can come up with solutions for the sake our country." Conservatives need to do the same. Trash the emails and engage. Don't send your liberal acquaintances emails that you know are going to make them mad, invite them to dinner and make friends. It's the Noisemakers that are the enemy. Liberals know something is wrong, they just need to see conservatives as good people. Be that person. Madness is doing the same thing and expecting a different result. Conservatives and liberals need to try something new. If the Noisemakers win, both conservatives and liberals lose.

Everybody has a desire to feel secure. Security in any system means basic food, shelter and clothing. If you think that you have a "right" to it, then you need to realize that someone else has to give these things to you. Something has to produce it. If government is the answer, remember you are the government. If you think about it that way, you still have to give it to yourself, plus overhead and taxes. In the capitalist and competitive system, dollars are created from nothing. These created dollars provide basic needs but in a more spiritually rewarding way. For a man to achieve and grow is a positive thing. When you passively take from others, you are spiritually de-motivating yourself and taking yourself down a path that is backwards. Passive receipt of what you need instead of active creation of it is self-destruction. It's hard to feel proud of yourself when you are not accomplishing on your own. True pride is what you have accomplished. If you are only taking things from other people, are you not a thief by virtue of forcing the government to take money from someone else and not giving yourself the opportunity you need to become a positive growing human being?

Become engaged. Stay away from the affinity groups that you agree with all the time. If you only listen to those who spout dogmatic jargon that you like to hear, you have no grounding to know if it's based in facts until you can engage with both sides. I asked a relative of mine if she had read Rush Limbaugh's book; "No," she said, "I'm not interested. I've never listened to his show. I've heard from reliable people that he's a racist."

I said, "I will read Al Gore's book and you read Rush's book and we'll talk about it." She was unwilling. It makes me question that she might discover that he had some good things to say. It boiled down to an argument between me and her. She used irrational justification to not read the book; also, it would be satisfying to me. I was more than willing to read Al Gore's book. I did read it. I read Saul Alynsky's book, *Rules for Radicals*. I didn't agree with it. I thought that it was a Noisemaker book about how to control people. At least I know what he's thinking and I can formulate my own ideas with that understanding.

I did that with my childhood friend. I would send him emails that were contrary to his point of view. He was also getting the same thing from his other friends. Whenever I asked him to tell me his opinions, he would give me answers from some other source. I said, "Send me your ideas. Here's my opinion." I've asked him a dozen times and he's never given me his own opinion even one time. Our arguments digress to which source is credible and which is not. Finally, I said to my friend, "Let's just be like when we were Boy Scouts and we were discussing matters of the universe as young people do. We would discuss anything. There was nothing too nutty. "Let's have a *kum ba ya* moment." I said I wanted to know what he thought and not what others thought. My friend just shut down. He is afraid, I realized, of being beaten up and attacked. It's important when you talk about political and social ideas to realize that they are ideas and it is a discussion. Whether or not someone agrees with you should not dictate whether or not you treat them with kindness, compassion and tolerance. You may believe that all of politics can be decided by the abortion issue. Your brother may believe that abortion should be a legal right. He's your brother and so is everyone else you engage with and that fact trumps your emotional desire to lash out. The more abortion is talked about, the fewer there have been. Civility creates an open atmosphere for thought. The Noisemakers know this and will try to keep the two sides apart. We can nullify them by understanding.

You want to make things work? Then exercise self-discipline and adult discretion as you engage with others regarding politics and the economy.

Refusal to listen to, or read or even try to understand other viewpoints is a dangerous cocoon. Such a mindset is like an addictive behavior of denial, justification and rationalization. This narrow way of thinking leads to your depression and it even leads to economic depression if enough people participate in it. Do you want gridlock? Many of us want congressional deadlock because we understand the less they do the better. We just don't want America to stand still. Do you want America to stand still? That's what you're creating when you hibernate with your own world view. Liberal, conservative or radical, if you are surrounding yourself with people who agree with you, then you're not that different from an addict. You're hurting yourself.

Why not give it a shot? Do it in a comfortable atmosphere. Today, you have to be careful about the information you read because many times it is not true. Drill down on the Web sites you find and discover the source. Is it a blogger or a self-appointed expert? What do the scientific studies show? What does the opposing side think? Everyone should watch all of the channels, including Fox. Fox happens to be the only channel you can listen to that is not in the bag for an ideology. Why do you think they are so demonized?: Must be a threat to someone. You may not like what you see and how it is said, but suffer through what they say and then sit and think about it.

There are people who don't have your best interest at heart and prey on some more than others. When you are walking in the woods, wear star spangled hats. Wave your flag! Lenin called people who would not engage and would not listen, "useful idiots[3]." Don't be a useful idiot who is shot and stuffed and hanging on a Noisemaker's wall! The only way tyranny can exist is that the people allow it. Today, we have stepped so far away from the vision of the Founding Fathers where most of the power rested with the states. We are at the pinnacle of centralized control and will go one way or the other. People need to think about what more centralized government will mean to their success. In my opinion, it means their destruction and their lives will get worse, because they cannot get better. At the root of all government is the self-discipline and careful choices of its citizens.

Look what happened in the Soviet Union, in New York state, Michigan, New Jersey, and California. People are moving out and whole states are becoming bankrupt[1]. The Noisemakers will be there to rescue them with your money and thereby seize control by default. We need to understand and think about what we're doing. This is not about getting mad, it's about standing tall as United States citizens. No matter what your heritage is, you are here because it is a system that works better than any other. What are you going to do to keep it? What is going to work for us as individuals begins with our family unit and expands as we become more successful. The genius of capitalism is that you can own every company without working in any of them, as I explained in the previous chapters on investment. We're blaming the capitalist system when the fault lies within us. Ouch!

We are not engaging each other and trying to convince each other in a simple way, but by screaming at each other. How's that working for you? Do you want to act like a bunch of gorged, greedy politicians or do you want to act like reasonable people of conscience and humanity?

An individual doesn't have enough money to buy into 400 different real estate deals, but as a group we can. An individual can't take a computer he invented to the world market, but by relying on a group, he can. An individual can start a business, but without appealing to the group he has no one to sell it to. We need to be individuals because we have unique skills, but when we hand our ideas to a group that we can choose in which to invest, we elevate them beyond comprehension. If we fall prey to the Noisemakers' fear talk, they control everything, especially our belief in ourselves. Then we will be a non-functioning group dependent on a small group of people who are not concerned about our welfare. Sounds like prison.

We could get further today if we were more civil to one another. It is very hard for me as it is for you, but we must! The leaders are always going to be the same until we demand that they be different. There are those who want to work toward the Founding Fathers' vision and others who want to take away our rights by giving us new rights, i.e., the right to healthcare, to own a car or house. This can never end except in eventual total destruction by ourselves or our foreign enemies. These are false prophets "giving" you something when they are actually taking far more away from you.

Noise Level Check: Chapter 7

1. Who is the one person in your life who disagrees with your world view the most?

2. Would you be willing to sit down and really listen to their point-of-view?

3. What does each of the members of your family think about the government's role in healthcare?

4. What were you taught in school about how to influence your elected leaders?

5. What is an activist?

6. What is a radical?

7. What books have you recently read by people with whom you disagree? Can you see how they came to their conclusions?

Do you have additional thoughts you would like to share with me about this chapter, or questions? I want to know what you think! Email me at steve@thenoisemakersbook.com

In reality there is perhaps
no one of our natural Passions so hard to subdue as Pride.
Disguise it, struggle with it, beat it down, stifle it,
mortify it as much as one pleases, it is still alive,
and will now and then peek out and show itself.

~ Benjamin Franklin, Autobiography, 1771

Avoiding

the

Noisemakers

It's a simple phrase, "Avoiding the Noisemakers," but if you really take it apart, it's anything but simple. First of all, you can't actually avoid hearing Noisemakers, but you can avoid believing them. They're imbedded in government and in positions of power. In fact, smaller versions of Noisemakers are in every community, church and business. These are essentially people who decided at a certain point that having position, prestige and power made them important. Then, from that decision, they made the logical leap to the conclusion that being important was all that mattered. I say "logical" leap and I'm referring to emotional logic, not intellectual.

When it comes to being important, we're all important the day we are born. We are sacred in and of ourselves. There is nothing we can say or do that will make us more important. The importance I'm referring to here has to do with who we are as spiritual beings, souls in this world. I am not referring to how much people like us or don't like us at any given moment, or how many awards we have stowed on our mantle. These are passing accolades that really don't mean much. What matters the most in life is being true to yourself and then living in integrity with the people around you. You don't demonize others because they committed a sin. We all are sinners. As Jesus said, "He who is without sin cast the first stone[1]." We have become a society of the self-righteous. Just because Clinton did what he did does not make him evil, just human. Nixon was not evil because of Watergate. They are human. The vitriol we are seeing today means that good people who have made mistakes are kept from serving. We think we must be perfect and if we are perfect we are not human. God does not grade all sins, but I think he grades some. You better not harm his young children. Evil is very strong. Humans are weak. King David had a "few" very bad sins, yet he was a great leader. God does not judge us until the end, maybe we should take His cue. Evil will always attack the ones who desire to be righteous the hardest. Why do you think the Catholic church has such a hard time? Spiritual warfare is real. There is good and there is evil.

Both liberals and conservatives are religious. Noisemakers appear to be, but they secretly are their own demigods. They worship themselves through the state. The state or the party is not of itself, they are the state and they demand your all. They must demonize, distort and humiliate religion. They are clever and you must pay particularly close attention. This *is* rocket science.

A Noisemaker is like the kid who never realized their own inherent importance as a soul. Maybe they experienced a violent trauma as a child or maybe they were just ignored. Deep down, they felt invisible at an important time during their development. When they discovered the feeling of relative importance that having a title, winning an award and having a lot of money gives you, they didn't just enjoy it, wearing it like a new coat for a while. They ingested it, they absorbed it, and they melted it onto their bodies until they were the title, the award and the money. Noisemakers aren't stable people, but in their own emotional way, they have found identity.

It's important to understand and even to have compassion for one's enemy. Remember, they don't really understand you, nor have compassion for you. They have narcissistic world views, so you exist only in relation to them and their goals. Hitler was a Noisemaker on the right; Stalin was a Noisemaker on the left. I don't know about Stalin's early life, but I do know that Hitler exhibited disturbingly cruel behavior at a young age. Though they were monsters underneath, both men were charismatic leaders who electrified nations, leading trusting citizens and their governments into deep death spirals.

At the time, it was almost impossible to convince regular German or Russian voters that these electric, passionate men were lost inside of their own delusions. How could you sit down and explain it to them? That is exactly the challenge that you and I face today. How can we communicate the concept of the Noisemaker to the regular people around us? How can we bring a level of awareness into the citizenry of this country so that we too do not end up in a deep death spiral?

We have to relate to each person in a different way, depending on their point-of-view. The categories are: conservative, liberal, rich, middle class, CEO, small businessman, parents and kids. These are the people you have to reach one at a time.

Let's start with the parent. As I write this book in 2010, the Texas Textbook Commission has proposed eliminating historical references before the 1880's. Why? The time period before that discusses the Constitution and the founding of this country. It includes a study of the Federalist Papers. Eleven years ago, my own daughter's public school textbook had a chapter on communism and a short paragraph on capitalism. In the 1930' the Nazi's burned books that didn't fit the Nazi philosopy. Even teachers and students participated. In today's America they can never get away with that so they take the stealth route and just try to change books and teach their own warped views.

By using this kind of example, we can begin to show the steely manipulation by the Noisemakers to achieve their ends: power. That is their end. Nothing comes after it except our end. It isn't a three-dimensional goal. Once they achieve power and control, then they enjoy it and die, leaving us without a workable government, a solvent economy or any control over our own standard of living, e.g., Soviet Union, Cuba, the Eastern Block, Japan, Germany, Iran. Look what is happening in Venezuela. There will always be another one! But if it happens to America, the world will plunge into a dark era we cannot even imagine. Many of these countries would not even exist today if it weren't for the goodness of America. We are the shining light on the hill.

The first step in controlling the citizens of a country is to control the information that the children are taught. When young children can be brainwashed, then they do the work for the Noisemakers. In fascist and communist countries, children routinely turn their own parents into the authorities. They are brainwashed in school. Pol Pot even influenced children to kill their own parents in Cambodia[3]. Germany had the Hitler youth. Kids are born with no rules and will believe literally anything.

When my eldest daughter was in middle-school, she came home selling t-shirts to save the environment from the Nature Conservancy. I looked the Nature Conservancy up and called them to find out exactly what they are and what activities they are involved in. I discovered that the Nature Conservancy is a nonprofit political action group. They were buying up rainforest in Central America so farmers can't farm it. (I find this appalling from the fact that they are a left-wing political action committee working out of the public schools.) I called the teacher and asked if she knew she was raising money for a political nonprofit (PAC).

She told me, "Yes, I know that." I was dumbfounded. I called the principal and got the same reaction.

I said, "Well, I want to raise money for the Boy Scouts."

He said, "You can't do that!" He was shocked that I wanted to use schoolchildren for this. I asked him to explain the difference between what he was doing and what I wanted to do as they were both non-profits. He said, "Well, well, uh you just can't do that."

I called the Superintendent of the Schools. I told him what the teacher was doing and what the principal had said. The Superintendent said, "You're kidding! We'll stop that right now." I naively thought that the issue would go away.

After some time had passed, I learned that the sale of Nature Conservatory t-shirts was still underway. The Superintendent, it turned out, could not halt the process once it was underway; sentiment was so high among the students and teachers. In fact, the teacher actually chastised my daughter in front of the class and told her that her dad was ruining it for the class. My kids were horrified that I embarrassed them.

My point is that the schools are quietly, secretly training these kids to be left-wing socialists. Last week, FOX News interviewed a kid who said that he had "straightened" his parents out. One of the girls in the piece said, "It's like I was the parent and they were the child, but I

got them straightened out." Millions of young people have been taught
that everyone gets a trophy and there shouldn't be any winners or
losers.

I asked my other daughter, "Do you think that the environment
today is cleaner or dirtier than it used to be?"

This is an extremely bright 25-year-old (who is going to kill me
now by the way). She said, "Oh it's much dirtier." In fact, today's environment is probably cleaner than it's been since the 1830's when there
was garbage and refuse everywhere. That was the year that the
Cuyahoga River caught fire[.]. Today's schools are teaching kids that it's
dirtier than it's ever been. I remember how dirty the Mississippi River
was when I was growing up. I remember when hog processing companies and other industries were directly releasing refuse into our rivers. I
was right in there demanding that they stop. I still am. But it has gone
way beyond that goal now. It is a control method now. I do not know
the eventual goal of the Noisemakers wearing green hats has it beyond
reason to the point of nuttiness. Be worried. Al Gore is on TV saying,
"You as young people know things that your parents don't know."

Kids are saying, "We're more educated, more technologically
savvy than our parents. They've run up our debt. They are intentionally
destroying the economy and the environment. We have to vote for a
young savior to save us all from the rich."

As a parent, consider how the Noisemakers are affecting your children. Go to reliable sources and reeducate them. Teach them to question what they hear as the truth in school. Teach them both sides, but explain which one works. Tell them what is going on. They are not going to like it, because it may be contrary from what they are taught at school, but tell them anyway. Try to put the right people on the school board, but realize they are sent off to the state for "training." The education system controls itself. Why do you think the Noisemakers dislike charter schools even when parents are for them? If they can, THEY regulate them so they mirror the public system! Noisemakers must control information. Their system does not work and they must hide it. Noisemakers rarely send their kids to government schools. Go check.

Glen Beck is doing a remarkable job teaching history and exposing some Noisemakers. Watch with your kids and discuss. I noticed that history and government changed to sociology and sociology became the tool of the Noisemakers. So give your kids the game Sim City. When Noisemakers say we all have a right to this or that, reframe the question to a reality-based question: "Do you want to pay for someone else's healthcare who is perfectly capable of paying for their own? Are healthcare costs causing us financial hardship as someone presupposes? Is the dirty environment causing us hardship as asserted? Starting with a false premise backed up by false information is what Noisemakers do. It facilitates central control.

You can control young people by indoctrinating them, but why can't you just as easily get them to think the right way? When talking to young people, appeal to their natural skepticism and intelligence. Yes, it does sound so popular that we're destroying the environment and that the corporations are all corrupt. Is there a way to show them that the real corruption is the government itself? You can rely on simple facts: The US Post Office is seven billion dollars in the hole. Amtrak is broke, Social Security is bankrupt and Medicare is bankrupt. There is not one government program that ever paid for itself. The drug benefit was supposed to cost 400 million dollars, but will cost one trillion; you know, little details like that.

Challenge them to find just one government entitlement program that solved the problem it was intended to solve and cost what was advertised. Won't happen. The Federal Drug Administration – doesn't work. Financially it costs more than it should and doesn't solve the problems that it's supposed to solve. The Federal Aviation Administration doesn't work. Our planes cost 10 times more than they should because every part has to go through a long approval process for every tiny little part. If the market for a part is small, manufacturers will not even try.

The same holds true for drugs. There is no incentive for any regulator to say yes because to say no avoids any mistakes. These people have no good reason to say yes and every reason to say no. Do you think Cessna wants to sell a defective airplane part to ruin their profits and subject themselves to lawsuits and open the door for their competition.

Go back and look at the tax story in Chapter Three. The reality of taxes alone should convince any young person that there is a serious wormhole that we are all being sucked into. I remember when my daughter got her first paycheck and she lamented on how much was taken out for taxes. I asked her what she expected and she said," But I'm just a kid!" Ah, reality sets in! Every time I hear a person say "I don't mind paying a little extra so we can all be insured" I just about die. They have no idea what the true consequences really are. We need to engage and talk it through!

The federal government spends millions and millions of dollars "protecting" our borders from the masses of Mexicans fleeing their poverty stricken, crime-ridden country (rather than staying and working for change). Nevertheless, tens of thousands manage to cross over each year. Once an illegal alien is in this country, we issue them a taxpayer identification number and tax all of their earnings, which are generally quite low. Within a short time, the IRS receives requests for taxpayer identification numbers for the dependent nieces and nephews, sisters, brothers and parents of the illegal alien. These people walked over the border to "visit" or snuck over. Some are still living in Mexico. For the most part, however, from sneaking across the border as a criminal, the illegal alien now has the US taxpayer footing the bill for the schooling and healthcare of his or her extended family, usually on a wage of between $8K and $16K a year. Hmm. Can you think of a more efficient way of spending the taxpayer's money? Can you think of a better way to do things?

Let's look at the Mexican-American population. I am not talking Hispanics or legal Americans from Mexico, only people who cheated and actually hurt and insult the true immigrants. I admire the Mexican-Americans who came here legally, learned English, took care of family and are devoted to God. However, modern-day illegals do this: When bills come up to limit access to education or healthcare for illegal immigrants, they mobilize. They walk with signs, call Congress and use their power as perceived voters. Well, that's good, but why didn't they mobilize in Mexico and demand a real government instead of a pack of aristocratic drug dealers and child sex ring operators? Why don't they mobilize in this country to demand that our government quit enabling the Mafia state that is now Mexico? Why don't they work to create a prosperous nation that they can call home? They don't seem to realize that the Noisemakers want them only for their vote and will dole out only enough to make them dependent and keep them in their place.

It's good to use the power of the citizen, but this is another case of Noisemakers playing off the sentiments of the people and the people not really questioning it. Mexicans say, "We want to run away and have a better opportunity somewhere else, let us." That sounds good, but there is no quick and easy solution to the cesspool that is Mexico and that Mexican citizens helped create by their passive willingness to run away from the problem. By refusing to take responsibility for their own country and demanding that the United States help them do that, they are falling into the hands of crime lords and government control on both sides: Talk about a death spiral!

Most people could work out a better way to solve a problem and they do, but then when they try to tell someone about it, they hit a brick wall. Once a practice has become government policy it becomes a law etched in the pocketbooks of bureaucrats. The government is robbing us through sheer corruption and incompetency. What are you going to do about it?

Ask any drug manufacturer why it costs so much to buy medicine and they will tell you that it's because of the certification process. When you look at a social program like single-payer healthcare, you have to analyze it logically. When you look at it without emotional blinders on, you can see that it simply can't work, won't work and will cost more than it's supposed to. Every government agency is over budget now. The United States Government hired 7,000 more workers in the Department of Agriculture this year. In a time when there are fewer and fewer farmers, why did they do this? Salaries in the federal government are $100K and over with greater frequency than in the private sector. The money to pay the government person has to come out of the private sector. What is the eventual result of that? Doesn't that mean that we have to go broke or that we all end up working for the government? If that happens, where will they get the money? Recycling? Not sure what you can make with ground-up useless dollars or will it be Euros or Rubles or Yen........???

When you're talking to your kids, remind them that their teacher isn't going to tell them that the nature of government is to infringe and destroy the rights of the people and it is the job of every citizen to stringently research and curb the excesses of government. Ask your kids to go back and read *The Federalist Papers* and figure out how we were founded. People may want to indoctrinate you into a belief. There can be no relaxing of our vigilance as citizens. We don't have the luxury of just "letting things run themselves." Remember the popular kids who ran your student council in high school? Well that's what you've got running the country. Marketing plans in empty suits. How does that work for you? No, I take it back, I think I would just as soon have our high school council running the show. They were pretty smart kids from Iowa. You may not have been so lucky. If you want something less like High School Musical and more like the United States Constitution, then you have to get up, read, think, talk and act with discipline and care.

Winston Churchill once said if you're young and not a little bit liberal you don't have a heart and if you're old and aren't conservative, don't have a brain. We're on a journey as individuals and as a nation. No one's perfect or right all the time. The important thing is to be engaged. If you're not engaged, then like buzzards smelling death from afar, the Noisemakers will begin to circle in for the feed.

How can we avoid Noisemakers when they're all around us now?

Accept that there are no "easy" solutions. Fizzy, sweet drinks make you fat and sick. They're not the real thing. They're sucking up your money and your health. Think before you decide that something easy and quick is going to solve the problem, even one as basic as thirst…or healthcare or civil rights, or getting a job. Look at me: I'm a child of the Sixties. When I left home I did many menial nasty jobs for a living. I was a bankrupt, guitar-playing musician. It was in the 60's and 70's. Whatever you are thinking, well the answer is, "Yes I did it." Now I'm a financial advisor telling you the same thing I might have said when I was a young man in the Sixties, "Don't trust the government, Man. Think for yourself. Get your head out of the box and out of your……." If you stick your head in the sand you leave an even bigger target.

When you hear something that sounds plausible and people are repeating it, stop. Don't just go with the flow. Examples that I've given in this chapter are that our environment is dirty, that everyone has a right to a home, free healthcare and that the government has our best interest at heart. You get the picture. Noisemakers make everything palatable and desirable: nobody wants a dirty environment, no healthcare, to retire poor or for old people to suffer. Noisemakers make it sound like they're going to fix problems, but they are going to make them worse. They are striving to satisfy their addiction and make you co-dependent.

It is happening now, as we speak: central control and power. Another good example of Noisemakers is the creeping absurdity of political correctness. What is political correctness, really? It is you learning how to give someone else the power to control your speech. Political correctness is plain old censorship. When you think about political correctness, it is an exercise in the absurd so that the somewhat absurd looks normal. Pretty soon your new normal is absurd. They've moved the bar. It's incremental the communist Chinese, the Marxists and the American Noisemakers have practiced incrementalism for years. The goal is to have complete and total control over your life.

We the People will not be ruled over. We will be governed fairlybut not ruled over, unless we are indoctrinated from a young age that it is normal to be ruled over. *Normal* is only a relative term to what you know. Children kidnapped at a young age by sex perverts feel remorse when they are taken out of the environment. Of course they do, they have been raised up to feel and believe that abuse is normal. Even a grown woman like Patti Hurst was fully indoctrinated by her captors in a short period of time. If you think that you're safe and you don't need to pay attention, you're wrong. In fact, you're shot and stuffed already.

Parents must read what is in the children's textbooks. If they question it or disagree with it, they must head down to school board meetings and cause a stink. They have to have the guts to organize and to fight the indoctrination if that's the case. We cannot expect that our kids will get a well-rounded education based on facts if they are being indoctrinated by the Noisemakers.

Today, they leave out debate as a part of the classroom learning process. The absence of debate is a form of indoctrination. My kids talked about it years ago. They said, "Guess what my teacher said today. How do I respond to that when we're not allowed to debate the issue in class?" If a college board and a college professor understand the history of communism and how they come to power, then they may allow for debate and open learning and discussion. Frequently, however, "political correctness" muzzles thought and speech on college campuses.

How can CEOs grasp the reality of Noisemakers and learn to avoid them? That's a tricky question since many CEOs are Noisemakers in their own organization or they are in cahoots with Noisemakers for their own personal gain. The CEOs have no risk in their profession. They will generally bend any way the government wants them to and not make waves. They would like to make a profit, but are successful even if they don't. If a corporation doesn't make money, it should be like a small business - the CEO should not get paid. They need to start learning that they can't sit back and not make money, let the whole thing go down the tubes and then take the next job and/or get bailed out by the government.

The CEO of Continental Airlines whom I mentioned earlier is a good example of a CEO making money while his company doesn't. Look at Jeff Zuckerman. He is the head of NBC which is losing money and yet media leaders are asking his advice on how to make money in media. The United States government is making deals with the media. NBC as a corporation has decided that the way to "make money" today is to get in bed with the government. Sound familiar? What happens when your objective journalists are getting their paychecks by being in the pocket of the government? Let's call up someone in the Soviet Union and ask them.

I said that CEOs of corporations "need to start learning that they cannot sit back and make money while a corporation is failing." I said that, and I'm asking you: Exactly how are they going to learn that? You're going to teach it to them, that's how. You and millions of other citizens of the United States of America are going to decide that when they get home from work, they're going to spend a little time blogging, writing emails to elected officials, meeting with others to debate and learn. Maybe you spend "quality time" with your kids at the end of the day or on the weekends. What better quality time than to learn how to think and run your own country as a true citizen.

You can also vote with your money. Where do you put your money? Put it with the small businessman. When you finish reading this book, you will know how to kick your useless financial advisor who is only pushing corporate stocks and bonds out the door.

The small businessman usually gets his money from the bank or from a few burdensome private equity firms. Let's give him more choices. Let's force the big firms to do it right. Let's force the big investment companies to do it right. Demand it! Demand that they offer more choices and that they think about you for a change. If you demand that there be more investment product out there, they will provide it or perish The reason we want to support small business is: 1) It's who we are and 2) If the small business CEO doesn't make a profit, they don't get paid. Their interests are aligned with yours. We need our stock and bond markets, but the more competition the better. We will force our corporations to make a profit. We will put business men and women in charge and not corporate politicians who have very little down side and who cow-tow to the Noisemakers.

If you are a small businessperson faced with the fiasco before us now, I want to tell you to keep going. Don't give up. Keep looking for money in different scenarios. For this economy to survive, we have to have "connectors" who keep linking people up with advisors and advisors who can point to good investment products. Eighty percent of all jobs need to be from small businesses raising money and not necessarily through banks.

We have to get this country back into manufacturing. The government must create a business environment that attracts and not repels. The whole world must want to come here as it once did. We need to attract the best. It is not happening any more. We must find ways to develop and fund manufacturing sector companies. Manufacturing is what made the United States the most successful in the last 30 years. Now since we can't increase salaries for workers because of a punitive tax system, corporations move offshore, and price protections and tariffs that have never worked are still not working.

If you are a conservative in this Age of the Noisemaker, then I would say to you that you need to start engaging liberals because you and liberals are the same. Liberals are not your enemy. They are your salvation. They could keep our charities running and keep us focused on helping one another (I know, Mr. and Mrs. Conservative; you support charities and volunteer, but maybe you could involve your new liberal friends.) Some of them have been fooled into thinking that that should be done by the government, like pastors who think their only real job is to preach a sermon. Get involved in helping and being of service to those in need. Cut through the stereotype of the conservative who lives in an exclusive community and controls his life with his money while complaining about how the poor act so bad and crazy. Get over yourself and be of service with your hands and your heart.

Liberals: engage and listen and think things through. Things don't happen in a vacuum. When you take money from one person to only give it involuntarily to another, it has a negative effect on you. Yes, the conservatives sound like they are mad at you. That's because you are locking up emotionally and don't like them. This is not an accident. You have to love someone before you will talk to them. They don't, but you do. Maybe you have AIDs and they have maids. Maybe you're concerned and they've been burned. Maybe they love their liberty and their country and you do, too. There's a common ground.

Try to develop trust.

Here's why we are the same: We all want our kids to have a good education. We all believe in the same things at our core: life, love, God, family, but we are letting the Noisemakers control the debate and frame the argument. We haven't realized that that's what's going on.

Think about how the systems work and see how the government

system isn't what you as a liberal want. In the Sixties, the sentiment was anti-war and anti-government. The favorite book was *1984* by George Orwell. Now you're going toward just such a society. Can you see it? We all need to be against Big Brother whether we are liberals or conservatives. Noisemakers are actively engaged in centralized control and takeover of the United States of America. They have framed the argument to make it look like they are fighting what they are actually representing. Now they want to rule over you.

For us to survive as a free nation we must lower taxes, decrease spending, put control back to the state and local governments, hold state and local governments accountable for civil rights violations, stimulate work by stimulating small business owners with low taxes and by becoming rich. We must praise profits and force our corporations to be responsible for them. Let competition be our regulators. There's plenty to go around if we're creating money rather than spending our own over and over again on inefficient and unnecessary government programs.

Noisemakers are destroying the human spirit. Ask yourself, "How good do I feel right now about things?" Listen to yourself, talk to yourself. I believe in you. We the People will not be ruled over. We have created our own government that has a constitution that works but we must have a renaissance of sorts to remember our roots. We must guard our personal liberties. The rest will take care of itself if we are free. This is my promise to myself. Will you take this journey with me?

Noise Level Check: Chapter 8

Write a letter to your grandchildren's grandchildren. Tell them about the kind of society and government you envision for them. Be realistic and take into account human nature and the patterns of change that you have observed in history and in your lifetime. How will spirituality influence the public sphere in 150 to 200 years? How will the contributions of your generation have made a difference?

If you'd like to save your letter for prosperity, wonderful! If you'd like to share it with me, I would love to read it. steve@thenoisemakersbook.com.

I love the man that can smile in trouble,

that can gather strength from distress,

and grow brave by reflection.

'Tis the business of little minds to shrink;

but he whose heart is firm,

and whose conscience approves his conduct,

will pursue his principles unto death.

~ Thomas Paine,

The American Crisis, No. 1, December 19, 1776

We Will Survive.

We Will Thrive.

There are no limits on anyone. You can achieve anything that you can believe and conceive and talk about. Decide what you want to become. Decide what you want to be as you take the next step. I'm going to set a goal so high that it seems like there's no way on earth that I can achieve it. That's the way that God has designed us but we hold ourselves back because of our injuries or perceived injuries and what other people tell us, and not paying attention to the world around us.

The biggest problem that we have right now is political. Politics can destroy dreams and alter goals forever. To be number one, you have to be the best you can be and you have to work for and with other people to make the world a better place. One of the American dreams is that we want our children to have it better than we do.

The Noisemakers in the United States right now are called "Progressives." At various times in history they have been known by different things: Franklin Roosevelt, Woodrow Wilson, Joseph Stalin and Pol Pot all came from a background of self-hatred. They turned their psychological injuries into a narcissistic grandiosity. They covered it well and made it sound the way their audiences wanted to hear it. Today's Noisemakers do the same thing. They want to fix things for you but it's only their way and you don't or won't like the outcome.

If you consider yourself a liberal today, think about who you are and what injuries you've sustained throughout your life. I challenge you to scrutinize the political leaders before you today. Are they who they say they are? The false prophets today are the opposite of who they say they are. Because you have learned to hate conservatives, you can't see who the false prophets really are. Conservatives yell and scream. They are portrayed by the Noisemakers as people who are radically self-interested people. What the Noisemakers have done is frame the argument so that your enemy is the conservative. Think about the environment, global warming, helping others. These are all trick phrases to use you as willing idiots to promote their agenda and take over your life. You are not idiots! Don't fall for it.

A good example of this is in the black communities in the inner cities. If what Noisemakers were saying was true, then these people wouldn't be in crime-ridden, drug-infested, hopeless neighborhoods. Over the years, the Progressives/Noisemakers have put them in deeper and deeper. Because you believe that conservatives hate black people and are racists, you don't see or hear what the progressive political leaders are really saying. By the way I have another name for these folks. I call them "Progs." People for the Repression Of Good. Don't be a PROG (Progressive sounds too good). It is their main trick. They call it a "movement." You can be a member in a movement. "Progressive" sounds like you are moving forward and becoming better, but in their typical fashion they have the opposite in mind.

If you are a conservative, you must realize that you are injured too. Everybody makes it through this life with some sort of emotional/psychological injury. You are not less emotional than a liberal, but you are less emotionally logical than a liberal. You can think things through, but you are less capable of expressing your feelings appropriately. You think you can influence a liberal by sending him or her an email about how smart you are and how dumb they are. Not!

You've got to change the dynamic because the liberals are not the enemy. They can help you achieve what you want to achieve, which is to charitably help your fellow man without going through the government. You want to do the same thing they want to do and you do it through charities, but you need to involve the liberals. We're all going to be led astray by the Noisemakers who call themselves "Progressives." They need you to be hated by the liberals and you are doing their bidding.

The angry rhetoric garbage you are sending to the liberals is from the Noisemakers. You're being manipulated. Go out and find liberals to hang around with. You will get frustrated and think they just don't get it. They want to love you, but they think you're an ape. Communicate on the level at which they live and learn what they have to teach you. Engage with them and have civil conversations and send them a poem and connect on levels that you have in common. Let them know in some way shape or form that you want the same things they want. That is, you want everyone to be rewarded and prosperous. You believe, as they do, that success is the progressive realization of worthy ideals, not just money. They need to connect with you on a personal level, not just online. Go where they are and have discussions not arguments. When you get in an argument with a liberal, to them, you become an emotional weirdo. Another 20% of the population has bought into the Noisemaker manifesto. The other 20% , who are defined as liberal, are open to new ideas.

What happens to the human spirit when it has to live in a polarized environment full of fear and hate? We are harming ourselves, whether we are liberals or conservatives when we fail to connect.

Noisemakers are there to lie, pervert, distort and destroy your spirit and do with you what they did with the people in inner cities: put you down and keep you down.

Then, whether you are a liberal or conservative, ask yourself how these people got there and how they can get out. Conservatives want people to get out and make money and be customers and liberals want people to get out and live abundant lives. Coming together as Americans, liberals and conservatives can turn this thing around.

We will not let the Noisemaker progressives turn us into a Western European, then socialist, then totalitarian government. In the wake of economic collapse, Noisemakers use the same methods. Their central control solutions become the answers to your problems. Their answers sound like one thing but they are not really what you want because the end result is loss of freedom and loss of wealth.

Ask the people who live in Eastern Europe, or the people in Western Europe who moved here. Ask the Canadians. We are not like Europeans. Our ancestors moved here because we are the entrepreneurs of the world. Our ancestors wanted little government because they knew that we fail when the government drives us with our own money.

The Noisemakers are driving us toward centralized control, all the while making it sound like you're going to have a clean environment and a wonderful life. You won't have to worry about food, shelter and clothing....healthcare. This manipulative approach will destroy you and your spirit and the possibilities of your children having it better than you did.

If we're united, conservatives and liberals against the Noisemakers, we can bring America back to the greatness that we were enjoying a few short years ago. We can still set the example that the rest of the world can follow. We don't want to go back to where the Europeans are; we want to lead them forward to where they should be. Europeans don't have the benefits that our poor class has. We need to bring our poorer classes up by bringing everyone up at the same time. Americans cannot be enemies of each other. We must band together to protect our capitalist economy and our democratic form of government. The Noisemaker progressives are socialists and Marxists on steroids.

A common enemy always works to create unity and the common enemy is the Noisemaker progressives.

Turn away from the lies out there on the Internet. Some immature types love nothing more than to throw these back and forth. How do you feel about that?

Instead, purposefully direct the conversation by saying, "Here are the same things that we want." This is the message of Rush Limbaugh, but liberals do not even listen to him at all. They are offended. How can one be offended by someone else's view? When you hear someone say that they have been offended, perk up your ears. They have been indoctrinated. I may not like what a person says, but I am rarely offended by a non-personal opinion, but I am by a personal insult. Glenn Beck is the opposite of a Nazi but the Noisemaker progressives have convinced liberals that that is what he is.

The devil is not going to look like the devil. He's going to seem like the nicest person you ever met as he steals all your money. Bernie Madoff was one of the nicest guys you would ever want to meet. The benefit of today's chaos and strife is that we have seen Noisemaker members of Congress and the President remove their masks. You have to add up the numbers. Let's make it so we fight and win this battle together and stand battle-ready to protect what we hold dear. I know liberals think that something is wrong. You are right.

We as Americans can do this. We have been manipulated, misled and robbed, but, by the grace of God, we are not yet shot and stuffed by the Noisemakers. We can survive. We can thrive. I am not a survivalist, I am a thrivalist: one step at a time.

Who is your guide? You are. We are. We are our own government. You are the voice raised in opposition. You are the peacemaker. You are the citizen of the United States of America. You are the creator of new wealth and new liberties. You.

Noise Level Check: Chapter 9

Write to me and tell me three things you are going to do every week to participate in your government. When you write to me, tell me what you will be replacing in that time slot and how you negotiated that change with yourself and others.

Each period of time that we spend matters, and each action replaces another, so tell me how you are consciously and reasonably taking action in the nitty-gritty aspects of your day-to-day life. steve@thenoisemakersbook.com.

Citizens by birth or choice of a common country,
that country has a right to concentrate your affections.
The name of American, which belongs to you,
in your national capacity,
must always exalt the just pride of Patriotism,
more than any appellation derived from local discriminations.

~ George Washington,
Farewell Address, September 19, 1796

END NOTES

Chapter 1

1. "The American Republic will endure until the day Congress discovers that it can bribe the public with the public's money." This is a variant expression of a sentiment which is often attributed to Tocqueville or Alexander Fraser Tytler, but the earliest known occurrence is as an unsourced attribution to Tytler in "This is the Hard Core of Freedom" by Elmer T. Peterson in *The Daily Oklahoman* (9 December 1951): "A democracy cannot exist as a permanent form of government. It can only exist until the majority discovers it can vote itself largess out of the public treasury. After that, the majority always votes for the candidate promising the most benefits with the result the democracy collapses because of the loose fiscal policy ensuing, always to be followed by a dictatorship, then a monarchy."

Source: http://en.wikiquote.org/wiki/Alexis_de_Tocqueville

2.   "Other sociological issues fueled the growth of the larger

counterculture movement. One was an influential nonviolent
movement in the United States which resolved
Constitutional civil rights illegalities, especially regarding
general racial segregation, the lack of voting rights among
Southern blacks, and the existing segregation in the purchasing
of homes or rental housing in the North.

On college and university campuses, student activists fought
for the right to exercise their basic Constitutional rights,
especially freedom of speech and freedom of assembly.

Many counterculture activists became newly aware of the
ongoing plight of the poor, and community organizers
fought for the funding of anti-poverty programs, particularly
within inner city areas in the United States.."

Anderson, Terry H. (1995). *The Movement and the Sixties.*   Oxford
University Press. ISBN 0195104579.

Hirsch, E.D. (1993). *The Dictionary of Cultural Literacy.*   Houghton
Mifflin. ISBN 0-395-65597-8. p 419.

"Members of a cultural protest that began in the U.S. in the
1960s and affected Europe before fading in the
1970s...fundamentally a cultural rather than a political
protest."

Jentri Anders, *Beyond Counterculture*, Washington State   University
Press, 1990, ISBN 0874220602 & ISBN 978-0874220605

3.   *Big Brother* is a term coined in the 1960's to refer to government authority and authority figures who sought to control the general population through force and sabotage of basic civil and human rights.

Orwell, George (1949). *Nineteen Eighty-Four*

4.   The United States Census Bureau considers a baby boomer to be someone born during the demographic birth boom between 1946 and 1964.

Landon Jones, who coined the term "baby boomer" in his book *Great Expectations: America and the Baby Boom Generation,* defined the span of the baby-boom generation as extending from 1946 to 1964, when annual births declined below 4,000,000. They have since returned to higher levels in the "echo boom."

Seventy-six million American children were born between 1945 and 1964, representing a cohort that is significant on account of its size alone. Baby Boomers control over 80% of personal financial assets and more than 50% of discretionary spending power.

U.S. Census Bureau — "Oldest Boomers Turn 60" (2006)
http://www.census.gov/Press-Release/www/releases/archives/
facts_for_features_special_editions/006105.html
Economy faces bigger bust without Boomers, Reuters, Jan 31,

2008http://www.reuters.com/article/ousivMolt
idUSN3131412220080131

5.   The study, which was released on May 25, 2007, emphasized
that in real dollars, this generation's men made less (by 12%)
than their fathers had at that same age in 1974, thus reversing a
historical trend. The study also suggests that per year increases in
the portion of father/son family household income generated by
fathers/sons have slowed (from an average of 0.9% to 0.3%),
barely keeping pace with inflation, though increases in overall
father/son family household income are progressively higher each
year because more women are entering the workplace,
contributing to family household income.

http://money.cnn.com/2007/05/25/pf/mobility_study
index.htm?cnn=yes

"Xers witnessed the rise of the yuppie and the burst of the
dot-com bubble. Theirs, he argues, was a bleak inheritance.
"Instead of getting free love, we got AIDS," says Douglas
Rushkoff, author of 1993's GenX Reader . "We didn't believe
the same kind of things as boomers. It was much harder to
fool us." Just as Xers shunned boomer notions, it seems
millennials have similarly turned against the Gen-X ethos.
"If the Gen-Xers were like 'No, I'm not in it for the money,'
millennials rebelled against that and are completely greedy,"
Gordinier says in a video he posted to YouTube about the
book.

http://www.time.com/time/arts/article/0,8599,1731528,00.html

6. "During the years of colonization, public relief was supported by individuals and groups who donated resources and labor to institutions such as schools and hospitals or directly to needy people. Much assistance to the form of neighborly kindness or mutual aid….Almshouses were not developed systematically but over the next 150 years they were established throughout the colonies as the need arose. The numbers of these houses made it increasingly obvious that there were large numbers of needy individuals that the towns could not support. With this trend began the trend for larger governmental units to accept the responsibility of the 'state poor.'

An Introduction to Human Service By Marianne Woodside and Tricia McClam © 2005, 2006 Thomson Brooks/Cole Belmont, CA

7. Jeremiah Alvesta Wright, Jr. (born September 22, 1941) is an American Pastor Emeritus and the former Pastor of the Trinity United Church of Christ (TUCC), a megachurch in Chicago with around 8,500 members. In early 2008, Wright retired after 36 years as the Senior Pastor of his congregation and no longer has daily responsibilities at the church. Following retirement, Wright's beliefs and manner of preaching were scrutinized when segments from his sermons were publicized in connection with the presidential campaign of Barack Obama.

One controversial sermon quotation, ""And the United States of America government, when it came to treating her citizens of Indian descent fairly, she failed. She put them on reservations. When it came to treating her citizens of Japanese descent fairly, she failed. She put them in internment prison camps. When it came to treating her citizens of African descent fairly, America failed. She put them in chains, the government put them on slave quarters, put them on auction blocks, put them in cotton field, put them in inferior schools, put them in substandard housing, put them in scientific experiments, put them in the lowest paying jobs, put them outside the equal protection of the law, kept them out of their racist bastions of higher education and locked them into positions of hopelessness and helplessness. The government gives them the drugs, builds bigger prisons, passes a three-strike law and then wants us to sing 'God Bless America.' No, no, no, not God Bless America. God damn America — that's in the Bible — or killing innocent people. God damn America, for treating our citizens as less than human. God damn America, as long as she tries to act like she is God, and she is supreme. The United States government has failed the vast majority of her citizens of African descent..."

http://www.tucc.org/pastor.htm

Ramirez, Margaret (2008-02-11). "Barack Obama's former pastor, Rev. Jeremiah Wright Jr., preaches last sermon at Trinity United Church of Christ". Chicago Tribune. http://

www.chicagotribune.com/news/local/chi-wright_11feb11,1,4431179.story. Retrieved 2008-03-22.

"Tell the Whole Story FOX! Barack Obama's pastor Wright". Excerpted from YouTube. http://youtube.com/watch?v=RvMbeVQj6Lw. Retrieved 2008-03-25.

8.   Economic prosperity of the 1950's:

In 1950, the country's GDP was at $293.8 Billion (in current dollars). At that time, Per Capita GDP was $9,573.00 - making the United States the number one country world wide in this aspect. By 1996, GDP was at $13.194 Trillion. Per Capita GDP was at $43,800.00 - however, the country ranked only at 10th place world wide in this respect.
In 1950, the civilian labor force was about 58 million strong. Only 5.3 percent of the labor force was unemployed. 41.6 million of the labor force at that time were males, while only 17.34 million were females.

In 1950 the Per Capita Personal Income was pegged at $1,501.00. By 2006 this rose to about $36,600.00. Though marked by huge difference in amount, it can be noted that $1,501.00 in 1950 could by more goods and services than the $36,600 in 2006 as illustrated by the CPI rates for both years.

Article Source: http://EzineArticles.com/?expert=Carlo_Simbajon

9.   Moral Decline since the 1950's:
"You can point to the '60's, when there began a deliberate

attempt to expunge God and moral absolutes from schools, government buildings and the culture in general. Because of that, you now have a drifting people who don't really know who they are or what they believe, so they fill the void by pumping in all kinds of garbage. The Chronicle of Higher Education says more and more 17- and 18-year-olds are coming to colleges as freshmen depressed, on psychotropics, feeling lost and valueless. When you raise an entire generation in a relativistic, purposeless world where there is no living God, people drift around aimlessly."

~ Dr. James Dobson http://www.pluggedin.com/familyroom/articles/ 2008 achatwithrebeccahagelin.aspx

"The growth of government has politicized life and weakened the nation's moral fabric.

Government intervention—in the economy, in the community, and in society—has increased the payoff from political action and reduced the scope of private action. People have become more dependent on the state and have sacrificed freedom for a false sense of security."

~ James A. Dorn Cato's Letter #12

The Rise of Government and the Decline of Morality by James A. Dorn, Copyright © 1996 by the Cato Institute

10. "Individuals, groups and nations — if rational and self-interested — will equalize the marginal returns of two main

ways of generating income: 1) production combined with mutually advantageous exchange, versus 2) political or military distributive struggles. In such struggles it might be expected that initially stronger or richer contenders would grow ever stronger and richer still, but the reverse often occurs (Paradox of Power)..."

"Do the Rich Get Richer and the Poor Poorer? Experimental Tests of a Model of Power " Research paper by Yvonne Durham, University of Arkansas

Jack Hershleifer, University of California at Los Angeles

Vernon L. Smith, University of Arizona   Working Paper #770

Department of Economics, University of
 California, Los Angeles Bunche 2263 Los Angeles, CA 90095May 1997
http://www.econ.ucla.edu/workingpapers/wp770.pdf

11.   Saul David Alinsky (January 30, 1909 – June 12, 1972) was an American community organizer and writer.

" Camouflage is key to Alinsky-style organizing. While
 to build coalitions of black churches in Chicago,
 Obama caught flak for not attending church himself. He
 became an instant churchgoer.."

"Barack Obamas Unlikely Political Education"
The Agitator by Ryan Lizza Post date: 03.09.07 Issue date: 03.19.07

"That Hillary Clinton and Barack Obama share an Alinskyite background tells us two things. First, they are leftists, dedicated to overthrowing our Constitutional system. Second, they will go to any length to conceal their radicalism from the public.

"That is the Alinsky method. And that is today's Democratic Party."

By Richard Poe   1-13-2008

http://www.rense.com/general80/fon.htm

12.   Carbon Cap: Who Supports It?

"Cap and trade is the politically feasible and effective approach to solving the global   warming crisis. As a result, cap and trade enjoys the support of a broad array of leaders in business, government and the environmental community."
~ Environmental Defense Fund

Posted: 30-Jan-2009; Updated: 27-Jan-2010

http://www.edf.org/article.cfm?contentID=9138

13.   April 2010 Employment Situation Summary

Released Friday, May 7, 2010

Nonfarm payroll employment rose by 290,000 in April, the unemployment rate edged up to 9.9 percent, and the labor   force increased sharply, the U.S. Bureau of Labor Statistics reported today. Job gains occurred in manufacturing, professional and business services, health care, and leisure and hospitality. Federal government employment also rose, reflecting continued hiring of temporary workers for Census 2010.

Household Survey Data

In April, the number of unemployed persons was 15.3 million, and the unemployment rate edged up to 9.9 percent. The rate had been 9.7 percent for the first 3 months of this year.

Among the major worker groups, the unemployment rate for whites (9.0 percent) edged up in April, while the rates for adult men (10.1 percent), adult women

(8.2 percent), teenagers (25.4 percent), blacks (16.5 percent), and Hispanics

(12.5 percent) showed little or no change. The jobless rate for Asians was 6.8 percent, not seasonally adjusted.

The number of long-term unemployed (those jobless for 27weeks and over) continued to trend up over the month, reaching 6.7 million. In April, 45.9 percent of unemployed persons had been jobless for 27 weeks or more.

~ Bureau of Labor Statistics

http://www.bls.gov/news.release/empsit.nr0.htm

14.   "We are five days away from fundamentally transforming the United States of America"

Barack Obama October 31, 2008...1:20 pm University of Missouri

15.   "Paternalism refers to an attitude or a policy reminiscent of the hierarchic pattern of a family based on patriarchy, that is, there is a figurehead.(literally meaning 'father like')., pater in Latin) that makes decisions on behalf of others (the "wife" and "children") for their own good, even if this is contrary to their wishes.

It is implied that the fatherly figure is wiser than and acts in the best interest of its protected figures. The term may be used derogatorily to characterize attitudes or political systems that are thought to deprive individuals of freedom and responsibility, only nominally serving their interests, while in fact pursuing another agenda which is directly against the interests of the individuals."

"Another important component of psychological liberation was to embrace blackness by insisting that black people lead movements of black liberation. This meant rejecting the fervent "non-racialism" of the ANC in favor of asking whites to understand and support, but not to take leadership in, the Black Consciousness Movement. A parallel can be seen in the United States, where student leaders of later phases of SNCC, and black

nationalists such as Malcolm X, rejected white participation in organizations that intended to build black power. While the ANC viewed white participation in its struggle as part of enacting the non-racial future for which it was fighting, the Black Consciousness view was that even well-intentioned white people often reenacted the paternalism of the society in which they lived. This view held that in a profoundly racialized society, black people had to first liberate themselves and gain psychological, physical and political power for themselves before "non-racial" organizations could truly be non-racial."

Excerpt from the essay: "The Sharpville Massacre Its Historic Significance in the Struggle Against Apartheid" by David M. Sibeko

Biko, Steve. *I Write What I Like* University of Chicago Press (2002). The roots of conflicting consciousness is discussed in the introduction to this collection of Biko's writings as written by Lewis R. Gordon (see page ix), as well as in Chapter 11, Steve Biko's essay "Black Racism and White Consciousness" (pages 61-72), of that volume.

16.   Constitutional mandate for smaller government:

"The executive Power shall be vested in (only) a President of the United States of   America. He shall hold his Office during the Term of four Years, and, together with the Vice-President chosen for the same Term, be elected..."

Article 2, Section 1, The Constitution of the United States

"Added as an afterthought but today very much a key part of the American Constitution is the Bill of Rights. After enumerating specific rights retained by the people in the first eight amendments, the Ninth Amendment and the Tenth Amendment summarily spelled out the principle of limited government. Together, these two last Amendments clarify the differences between the unenumerated (as well as enumerated) rights of the people versus the expressly codified delegated powers of the federal government. The Ninth Amendment codified that the rights of the people do not have to be expressly written in the Constitution (i.e., do not have to be enumerated) to still be retained by the people.   In the reverse, though, the Tenth Amendment codified that any delegated powers of the federal government are only authorized to be performed so long as such delegated powers are expressly delegated to the federal government specifically by the U.S. Constitution.

The U.S. Constitution limits the power of the government in several ways. It prohibits the government from directly interfering with certain key areas: conscience, expression and association. Other actions are forbidden to the federal government and are reserved to state or local governments."

Barth, Alan, 1991, *The Roots of Limited Government,*

Ninth Amendment: "The enumeration in the Constitution, of certain rights, shall not be construed to deny or disparage others retained by the people. "

Tenth Amendment: "The powers not delegated to the United States by the Constitution, nor prohibited by it to the States, are reserved to the States respectively, or to the people."

The Constitution of the United States of America

17.   Millons in banker bonuses:

(CBS) KROFT: Do you think that's why they paid it back specifically?

PRESIDENT OBAMA: I think in some cases that was a motivation. Which I think tells me that the people on Wall Street still don't get it. They don't get it. They're still puzzled, why is it that people are mad at the banks. Well,   let's see. You guys are drawing down $10, $20 million bonuses after America went through the worst economic year that it's gone through in decades, and you guys caused the problem. And we've got ten percent unemployment. Why do you think people might be a little frustrated.

Transcript of *60 Minutes* Inteview of Barack Obama
December 7, 2009

http://www.cbsnews.com/stories/2009/12/13/60minutes/
main5975426_page3.shtml?tag=contentMain;contentBody

18.   Text of Fair Housing Act: http://www.justice.gov/crt/housing/title8.php

"The original Act was passed by the 95th United States Congress and signed into law by President Jimmy Carter on October 12, 1977 (Pub.L. 95-128, 12 U.S.C. ch.30).[38] Several legislative and regulatory revisions have since been enacted."

"CHICAGO, May 12— Racial discrimination and abuse by lenders of a Federal mortgage program are helping to create pockets of blight in black and Hispanic neighborhoods, according to a study of lending in the Chicago area.

The study, by the Chicago Fair Housing Alliance, an advocacy group, contends that lenders and real estate agents direct a disproportionate number of minority buyers to Federal Housing Administration loans. Since the loans are especially profitable for lenders, unqualified home buyers are given the loans and minority neighborhoods are pockmarked with the foreclosed homes of buyers who should never have been approved for the mortgage, the study concluded. "Were any private mortgage lending or mortgage insurance institutions engaged in activities with such clearly differential impacts for white and minority communities, HUD and the Department of Justice would surely file suit for discrimination under the Fair Housing Act," said Calvin Bradford, a fair-housing researcher who wrote the study, which was financed by the MacArthur Foundation. The study is to be released on Wednesday at a hearing of a

House housing subcommittee, where the study's author and others will testify…"

New York Times Article: "Home Loans Discriminate, Study Shows" By Bill Dedman Published: May 13, 1998 http://www.nytimes.com/1998/05/13/us/home-loans-discriminate-study-shows.html

19.   Legislative changes to the Fair Housing Act under Clinton 1999

In 1999 the Congress enacted and President Clinton signed into law the Gramm-Leach-Bliley Act, also known as the "Financial Services Modernization Act."

http://en.wikipedia.org/wiki/Gramm-Leach-Bliley_Act

20.   Massive use of credit in the United States

TOTAL CREDIT CARDS: 576.4 million

TOTAL DEBIT CARDS: 507 million

Average credit card debt per household with credit card debt: $15,788*

Total credit cards in circulation in U.S: 576.4 million, as of yearend 2009

Nilson Report, February 2010

Total debit cards in circulation in U.S: 507 million, as of yearend 2009

Nilson Report, February 2010

Average number of credit cards held by cardholders: 3.5, as of yearend 2008

"The Survey of Consumer Payment Choice," Federal Reserve Bank of Boston, January2010

Average APR on new credit card offer: 14.10 percent

CreditCards.com Weekly Rate Report, May 2010.

Average APR on credit card with a balance on it: 14.67 percent, as of February, 2010

Federal Reserve's G.19 report on consumer credit, May 2010

Total U.S. revolving debt (98 percent of which is made up of credit card debt): $852.6 billion, as of March 2010

Federal Reserve's G.19 report on consumer credit, March 2010

Total U.S. consumer debt: $2.45 trillion, as of March 2010

Federal Reserve's G.19 report on consumer credit, May 2010

U.S. credit card 60-day delinquency rate: 4.27 percent.

Fitch Ratings, April 2010

U.S. credit card default rate: 13.01 percent.

Fitch Ratings, April 2010

http://www.creditcards.com/credit-card-news/credit-card-industry-facts-personal-debt-statistics-1276.php

Chapter 2:

1. "…. In 1977, the Community Reinvestment Act
(CRA), aggressively lobbied for by ACORN and Jesse Jackson
Sr., passed. The purpose of that legislation was to punish
lenders for limiting loans to wealthier, more creditworthy
markets, a practice called "redlining" and to give regulators —
and the Department of Justice, no less! — the authority to make
life difficult for banks that didn't give loans to   politically
preferred pigmented folks. (The governor of my home state,
Deval Patrick, did much of this agitation when he was at the
Justice Department under Clinton.)

These activists concluded that disparate loan approval rates
between black and white borrowers was evidence of racism by the
banks against blacks because whites were approved for loans at
higher rates than black folk. Of course, had they looked at the
approval rates for Asians versus whites, they would have
concluded that the banking industry was racist against whites,
which is, to put it mildly, ridiculous. (For more, see Thomas
Sowell's *The Housing Boom and Bust.*)

During the 90s and early 2000s, activists, like Jesse Jackson and
ACORN, turned to the supposed housing gap between blacks and
whites and again, tried to get the banks to approve loans that
they really were in no position to give — so-called NINJA loans.
Jesse Jackson bragged about his involvement, pressuring those
banks in an ACORN "banking summit," in 1992. "Why did Jesse

James rob banks?" he asked, rhetorically, "Because that's where the money was."

Except from an article in the *Claremont Conservative* by Charles Johnson, December 30, 2009
http://www.claremontconservative.com/2009/12/jesse-jackson-srs-role-in-housing.html

2. " As *Wall Street Journal* reporter James R. Hagerty wrote two summers ago, 'For years, high-level jobs at Fannie Mae were lucrative prizes for lawyers, bankers and political operatives waiting for their next U.S. government post.' Now that the jig is up, let's meet some of the bipartisan warriors who fought for Fannie Mae's right to plunder."

"At the top of the list we must place Franklin D. Raines, chairman and chief executive officer of Fannie Mae from 1998 to 2004. Raines, who served as director of the Office of Management and Budget under President Clinton, had previously worked at Fannie Mae as vice chairman. Before that, he worked on the Clinton transition team following the 1992 election. Before that, he was a general partner at Lazard Freres & Co. Raines, as the Wall Street Journal reported, was forced to leave Fannie Mae in 2004, when regulators discovered it had broken accounting rules "in an effort to conceal fluctuations in profit and hadn't maintained adequate risk controls." The New York Times reported two year ago that regulators "have said that of the $90 million paid to Mr. Raines from 1998 to 2003 at least $52 million—more than half—was tied to bonus targets that were reached by manipulating accounting."

Raines agreed to a $24.7 million settlement with a federal regulator in exchange for charges being dropped, but he admitted no wrongdoing."

"Next up is Jamie S. Gorelick, whose official résumé describes her as "one of the longest serving Deputy Attorneys General of the United States," a position she held during the Clinton administration. Although Gorelick had no background in finance, she joined Fannie Mae in 1997 as vice chair and departed in 2003. For her trouble, Gorelick collected a staggering $26.4 million in total compensation, including bonuses. Federal investigators would later say that "Fannie Mae's management directed employees to manipulate accounting and earnings to trigger maximum bonuses for senior executives from 1998 to 2003." The New York Times would call the manipulations an "$11 billion accounting scandal. Gorelick, it should be noted, has never been charged with any wrongdoing.'"

"Fannie Mae and the Vast Bipartisan Conspiracy: A list of villains in boldface." By Jack Shafer Posted Tuesday, Sept. 16, 2008 on Slate.com
http://www.slate.com/id/2200160
Wall Street Journal quote taken from March 30, 2009 article:
http://online.wsj.com/article/SB123837208039067699.html

3.   Jesse Jackson and ACORN payback from FHA:

"A report from the board of Federal Home Mortgage Co., otherwise known as Freddie Mac, accuses the company of using a brokerage firm with close ties to Jesse Jackson as part of an effort to avoid taxes and skirt corporate accounting rules.

Blaylock & Partners, headed by Ron Blaylock, one of Jackson's Wall Street Project associates, was paid $250,000 by Freddie Mac to broker the report as the "Blaylock Trades."

According to the report, Blaylock began the series of trades in May 2000. The report concluded, "By structuring the trades through Blaylock, Freddie Mac avoided the higher tax burden associated with federal tax regulations."

The Blaylock & Partners trades began less than one month after Freddie Mac and Bank of America announced a $1 billion "joint campaign to increase home ownership among minority families" with Jackson's Rainbow/PUSH Coalition and his Wall Street Project.

The trades with Blaylock & Partners were just one aspect of the more than 100-page report that was released last Wednesday to investigate the company's accounting practices.

The McLean, Va.-based Freddie Mac also committed $1 million in April of 2000 "to help leverage the infrastructure of [Jackson's] Wall Street Project's 'One Thousand Churches Connected'" effort. The goal of the "One Thousand Churches Connected" project was to provide "economic literacy" to minority families and educate them on home mortgages. Jackson had criticized Freddie Mac in 1998 in a high-profile campaign that demanded the company end what he called "its racial discriminatory practices within the work environment and lending practices." He called on Freddie Mac shareholders to divest from the firm.

At least one Jackson critic believes the selection of Blaylock & Partners for the trades less than a month after Freddie Mac's announcement of a joint venture with Jackson is suspect.

"I doubt it's a coincidence," Ken Boehm, chairman of National Legal and Policy Center (NLPC), told CNSNews.com.

Boehm, whose NLPC filed a formal complaint regarding Jackson's finances with the Internal Revenue Service in 2001, believes that Blaylock's extensive involvement with Freddie Mac was the result of Jackson's "shakedown" of the mortgage giant.

"It's pretty clear there was a Jesse Jackson shakedown of Freddie Mac along the lines of his shakedowns of other major corporations, and once again, it appears that Blaylock has benefited from his close association with Jackson," Boehm said." Marc Morano, CNSNews.com, Tuesday, July 29, 2003

http://archive.newsmax.com/archives/articles/2003/7/28/ 134837.shtml

4.   John McCain fights funding of the FHA:

McCain - Federal Housing Enterprise Regulatory Reform
Act of 2005 (Democrats blocked reform)
Federal Housing Enterprise Regulatory Reform Act of 2005

Bill Summary

1/26/2005—Introduced. Federal Housing Enterprise
Regulatory Reform Act of 2005 - Amends the Federal
Housing Enterprises Financial Safety and Soundness Act of 1992
to establish: (1) in lieu of the Office of Federal Housing
Enterprise Oversight of the Department of Housing and
Urban Development (HUD), an independent Federal Housing

Enterprise Regulatory Agency which shall have authority over the
Federal Home Loan Bank Finance Corporation, the Federal Home
Loan Banks, the Federal National Mortgage Association (Fannie
Mae), and the Federal Home Loan Mortgage Corporation
(Freddie Mac); and (2) the Federal Housing Enterprise Board.
Sets forth operating, administrative, and regulatory provisions of
the Agency, including provisions respecting: (1) assessment
authority; (2) authority to limit nonmission-related assets; (3)
minimum and critical capital levels; (4) risk-based capital test; (5)
capital classifications and undercapitalized enterprises; (6)
enforcement actions and penalties; (7) golden parachutes; and (8)
reporting. Amends the Federal Home Loan Bank Act to establish
the Federal Home Loan Bank Finance Corporation. Transfers the
functions of the Office of Finance of the Federal Home Loan

Banks to such Corporation. Excludes the Federal Home Loan
Banks from certain securities reporting requirements. Abolishes
the Federal Housing Finance Board.

govtrack.us ^ | 1/26/2005 | Congressional Research Service

5.   Government interference in the banking industry:
"The monetary policy of the United States is the domain of the
Federal Reserve Bank and not the government. This process is in
direct contradiction of the U.S. Constitution that reposes the
responsibility of the monetary system with the Congress of the
United States. On April 27, 1936, hearings were held by the
House Committee on Banking and Currency. The preamble of
the bill - HR 9216 of the Seventy-fourth Congress, states, "The
committee had under consideration the bill (HR 9216) to restore
to Congress its constitutional power to issue money and regulate
the value thereof; to provide monetary income to the people of
the United States at a fixed and equitable purchasing power of the
dollar, ample at all times to enable the people to buy wanted goods
and services at full capacity of the industries and commercial
facilities of the United States; to abolish the practice of creating
bank deposits by private groups upon fractional reserves, and for
other purposes."
The Congress declared, "Whereas the permanent welfare of
the people and the protection of the economic life
of the   Nation are dependent on the establishment of a
monetary system wholly subject to the control of Congress that
will promote the interests of agriculture and labor, of industry,

trade, commerce, and finance for the economic well being of all citizens by the maintenance of an adequate supply of money with a unit of fixed average purchasing power, which will avoid excessive expansion or disastrous contraction." That preamble led to the body of the text.

"Section 1. That it is hereby declared to be the policy of Congress to provide such issuances of certificates of national credit as shall be requisite so to increase the purchasing power of the consumers of the United States as to make it conform to the capacity of the industries and people of the United States for the production and delivery of wanted goods and services, which capacity be declared to be the measure of national credit." The Congress attempted to issue non-interest bearing Treasury Notes. A Federal Credit Commission linked to the Secretary of the Treasury was the goal of Congress."

"Federal Reserve Controls the Money, Not the Government" By Harry V. Martin Copyright FreeAmerica and Harry V. Martin, 1995 http://dmc.members.sonic.net/sentinel/naij2.html

6.   Timothy Geithner indicted for tax evasion/fraud: "According to Mr. Geithner, he initially failed to pay payroll taxes on income he received from the International Monetary Fund in 2001, and then repeated the error in the three subsequent years, despite the help of an accountant. Apologizing to the committee, he took responsibility for what he called "careless" and "avoidable" mistakes while insisting they were unintentional. He acknowledged signing an IMF statement at the time that he

understood he had been reimbursed to pay those self-employ-
ment taxes, adding that he should have read the statement more
carefully. Millions Americans have said the same thing about the
tax code during an IRS audit, earning less forgiveness."

From an article in the *Wall Street Journal:* "Geithner's Tax Code:
The nominee explains his payment 'mistake.'" January 22, 2009 Author
Unknown

http://online.wsj.com/article/SB123258571706004547.html

Chapter 3

1.   General Motors bankrupcy:

On June 1, 2009, General Motors filed for Chapter 11 bankruptcy
proceedings, which were completed on July 10 of the same year,
and it was thereafter reorganized once a new entity acquired the
most valuable assets. GM is now temporarily majority owned by
the United States Treasury and, to a smaller extent, the Canada
Development Investment Corporation[5] and the government of
Ontario[6][7][8], with the US government investing a total of
US$57.6 billion under the Troubled Asset Relief Program.

Excerpt from an article, "Politicians Butt In at Bailed-Out GM",
on The WSJ.com, by Neil King, October 30, 2009.
http://online.wsj.com/article/SB125677552001414699.html.

2.   Continental Airlines losing money:

"...Continental jumped in size in 1987 by swallowing Frontier, People Express and New York Air.

Both airlines shrank to cope with the recession. United cut capacity 7.4 percent last year, and Continental shrank 5.2 percent.

And they've both been losing money. Continental reported a 2009 loss of $282 million as revenue plunged 17.4 percent to $12.59 billion. UAL lost $651 million for the year as revenue fell 19.1 percent to $16.34 billion.

Now we've got a company that can really clearly compete against Delta. Mergers are all about revenue, and this is a tremendous boost for revenue.

Article, "Continental, United To Form World's Largest Airline" by the Associated Press, May 3, 2010

http://www.npr.org/templates/story/story.php?storyId=126470639

3.   Canadian Premier comes to the USA for heart treatment:

"Recently, a Canadian Premier (their version of Governor) had a heart problem. He could of had free health care, if he waited long enough—but he decided he wanted to live instead. So he came to the United States for heart surgery.

An unapologetic Danny Williams says he was aware his trip to the United States for heart surgery earlier this month would spark outcry, but he concluded his personal health trumped any public fallout over the controversial decision."

Excerpt from an article in *California News and Views* by By Stephen
Frank, March 1, 2010 (A Republican Majority Campaign blog)

http://www.rmcpac.com/blog/canadian-politicians-pushing-health-
care-come-usa-heart-surgery

    4.   Greenspan "irrational exuberance" remark:

    [...] Clearly, sustained low inflation implies less uncertainty
about the future, and lower risk premiums imply higher
prices of stocks and other earning assets. We can see that in
the inverse relationship exhibited by price/earnings ratios
and the rate of inflation in the past. But how do we know
when irrational exuberance has unduly escalated asset values,
which then become subject to unexpected and prolonged
contractions as they have in Japan over the past decade? [...]

Remarks by Chairman Alan Greenspan
At the Annual Dinner and Francis Boyer Lecture of The American
Enterprise Institute for Public Policy Research, Washington, D.C.
December 5, 1996

The Federal Reserve Board text of the speech can be found here:

http://www.federalreserve.gov/boarddocs/speeches/1996/
19961205.htm

    5.   "In "Secret History of the Credit Card," FRONTLINE®
and *The New York Times* join forces to investigate an industry
few Americans fully understand. In this one-hour report,
correspondent Lowell Bergman uncovers the techniques used by

the industry to earn record profits and get consumers to take on more debt."   November 23, 2004

www.pbs.org/wgbh/pages/frontline/shows/credit/

Chapter 4

1.   Top 5% are paying 70% of the taxes:

"In 2007, the top 5% of income earners paid over half of the federal income tax revenue. However, as of 2004, the top 5% hold 59.2% of wealth. The top 1% of income earners paid 25% of the total income tax revenue."

Excerpt from an article, Spreading the wealth? U.S. already does it by Charles Babington, Associated Press, October 22, 2008, *Burlington Free Press*

  See also: http://www.ntu.org/tax-basics/who-pays-income-taxes.html

2.   Failure rate of small businesses:

"Failure Rates

Discussions of small business failure commonly include amorphous sets of numbers, intended to emphasize the enormity of the problem. Frequently, statements can be discovered suggesting that x percent of small businesses fail within y years. These percentages are usually high.

'. . . half of all small businesses fail within the first two years and 80 percent within the first five years

(*The National Times*, August 1980)

. . . about 70 percent of companies which start out with nothing will fail within two years.'"

Excerpt from an article, "Estimating the small business failure rate: a reappraisal", by Stephen Haswell and Scott Holmes; *Journal of Small Business Management*, Vol. 27, 1989

3.   Overtown, Miami riots:

"A police officer who touched off three days of racial violence when he shot a black man to death will not be charged with a civil rights violation, a Federal prosecutor said today.

Stanley Marcus, the United States Attorney here, said there was not enough evidence to bring the policeman, Luis Alvarez, to trial on Federal charges in the death of Nevell Johnson Jr., who was shot in a video arcade in Miami's predominantly black Overtown section on Dec. 28, 1982.

One person was killed and 26 were injured in three days of violence after the shooting. Officer Alvarez, 24, who said he had thought Mr. Johnson was reaching for a pistol, was acquitted March 15 of state manslaughter charges in the shooting of the 20-year-old man.

Officer Alvarez was suspended pending the end of the Federal investigation. His attorney, Roy Black, was unsure what his client planned to do next.

The article, "U.S. Won't Prosecute Officer Who Touched Off Miami Riots," UPI Published: September 12, 1984

4.   Rich people are a cancer to society:

"Is there anything to be said for 'the rich?'

"By that I mean anyone earning more than $200,000 a year (if single) or $250,000 (if married filing jointly), the new threshold established by the Obama administration for its tax increase proposals.

"With Bernie Madoff handcuffed and led off to prison last week (to the accompaniment of applause and tears of some of his victims), the rich seem to have reached a new low in popularity. Tabloid news sources are staking out resorts, luxury condos, airports for private jets, looking for any hints of indulgence or excess, especially if they involve taxpayer dollars. No wonder, given the stories emerging from the wreckage of the credit bubble."

Excerpt from an article, "Do the Rich Really Deserve Such a Bad Rap?", by James B. Stewart, SmartMoney.com, March 17, 2009.

SmartMoney.com http://www.smartmoney.com/investing/economy/do-the-rich-really-deserve-such-a-bad-rap/?hpadref=1#ixzz0p4ejYGpJ

5.   Walter Williams on restrictions to black entrepreneurs:

"There are hundreds of statutes that stifle competition and allow incumbents to charge higher prices. A taxicab license to own and operate one taxi in New York city has been as high as $160,000. High taxi license prices exist in other cities. License laws prevent people from hair braiding. There're license laws that prevent people from operating van services or even shining shoes. You might think that the "champions" of the little guy such as the U.S. Department of Justice's Anti-Trust Division, Urban League, NAACP, the Democratic party and black politicians would be in there fighting for the little guy's right to earn a living. You'd be absolutely wrong. If anything they are on the side of the powerful vested interests. That's the side on which their political/financial bread is buttered."

Excerpt from an essay, "Government and the Little Guy", by Walter E. Williams c47-00

October 13, 2000

http://econfaculty.gmu.edu/wew/articles/00/littleguy.html

6.   Thomas Sowell's Vision of the Annointed summary:

"If you're interested in reading about more bogus liberal myths that emerged in the 60s that were used to justify more government intervention and forced "social justice," read Thomas Sowell's Vision of the Anointed. It will completely change the mindsets of any open-minded person who still hangs on to the believe that prominent liberal public figures and other various and assorted left wing "do-gooders" don't massage and/or, in some cases, invent statistics in order to inject "change" into social and economic policy."

Excerpt from a blog, "The 'Poverty as the Root of Crime' Theory: Busted?" by Sister Toldjah on January 5, 2010 http://sistertoldjah.com/archives/2010/01/05/the-poverty-leads-to-crime-theory/

Chapter 5

1.Credit card late fees:

"Thirty-one of the 39 credit cards did not charge an annual fee. That marked a larger number of credit cards with no annual fee than in 2008, when 35 of 41cards had no annual fee. The cost of those fees ranged from $18 to $150. (Source: Consumer Action credit card survey, July 2009)"

http://www.creditcards.com/credit-card-news/credit-card-industry-facts-personal-debt-statistics-1276.php

2.   Mutual fund update publications:

CDA/Wiesenberger Mutual Funds Update (monthly)
CDA Investment Technologies, Inc.
1355 Piccard Drive, Suite 220
Rockville, MD 20850
(800) 232-6362
This publication provides detailed performance review and

analysis of mutual funds, money market funds, and closed-   end funds. The subscription price includes the annual   Panorama, a guide and directory to mutual funds, including 10   years of performance data.

Morningstar Mutual Fund Morningstar, Inc.

53 West Jackson Boulevard, Suite 460

Chicago, IL 60604

(800) 735-0700

www.Morningstar.com

Published every other week, and similar to the Value Line stock reports, this invaluable service delivers reports on individual mutual funds.

List of Value Line Products:

The Value Line Investment Analyzer® This software service provides professional stock analysis.

The Value Line Investment Survey® Online (Web) Powerful analytics allow users to manipulate numbers and ratios in ways never before possible.

The Value Line Mutual Fund Survey® for Windows® This data/software service includes extensive capabilities for viewing, sorting, screening, graphing, and preparing reports on mutual funds.

Interactive Daily Analysis and Rankings of more than 200,000 Stock and Stock Index Options .

The Value Line Convertibles Survey provides a systematic approach to assessing the performance of convertibles, ranking over 600 issues for potential risk and return.

Chapter 7

1.   Co-dependent definition:

"Co-dependents have low self-esteem and look for anything outside of themselves to make them feel better. They find it hard to 'be themselves.'" Some try to feel better through alcohol, drugs or nicotine - and become addicted. Others may develop compulsive behaviors like workaholism, gambling, or indiscriminate sexual activity.

"They have good intentions. They try to take care of a person who is experiencing difficulty, but the caretaking becomes compulsive and defeating. Co-dependents often take on a martyr's role and become "benefactors" to an individual in need. A wife may cover for her alcoholic husband; a mother may make excuses for a truant child; or a father may "pull some strings" to keep his child from suffering the consequences of delinquent behavior.

"The problem is that these repeated rescue attempts allow the needy individual to continue on a destructive course and to become even more dependent on the unhealthy caretaking of the "benefactor." As this reliance increases, the co-dependent develops a sense of reward and satisfaction from "being needed." When the caretaking becomes compulsive, the co-dependent feels choiceless and helpless in the relationship, but is unable to break away from the cycle of behavior that causes it. Co-dependents view themselves as victims and are attracted to that same weakness in the love and friendship relationships."

~ Mental Health America http://www.nmha.org/go/codependency

2.   The Ten Commandments text:

"And God spoke all these words, saying: 'I am the LORD your God...

1: 'You shall have no other gods before Me.'

2: 'You shall not make for yourself a carved image—any likeness of anything that is in heaven above, or that is in the earth beneath, or that is in the water under the earth.'

3: 'You shall not take the name of the LORD your God in vain.'

4: 'Remember the Sabbath day, to keep it holy.'

5: 'Honor your father and your mother.'

6: 'You shall not murder.'

7: 'You shall not commit adultery.'

8: 'You shall not steal.'

9: 'You shall not bear false witness against your neighbor.'

10: 'You shall not covet your neighbor's house; you shall not covet your neighbor's wife, nor his male servant, nor his female servant, nor his ox, nor his donkey, nor anything that is your neighbor's.'

The Bible, "Exodus" 20:2-17

3.   The term "useful idiots":

"The term is commonly attributed to Lenin, sometimes in the form "useful idiots of the West." to describe those Western reporters and travelers who would endorse the Soviet Union and its policies in the West. In fact, the earliest known usage is in a 1948 New York Times article on Italian politics. In 1987, Grant Harris, senior reference librarian at the Library of Congress, said "We have not been able to identify this phrase [useful idiots of the West] among [Lenin's] published works."

In political jargon, the term useful idiot was used to describe Soviet sympathizers in Western countries and the attitude of the Soviet government towards them. The implication was that though the person in question naïvely thought themselves an ally of the Soviets or other Communists, they were actually held in contempt by them, and were being cynically used.

The term is now used more broadly to describe someone who is perceived to be manipulated by a political movement, terrorist group, hostile government, or business, whether or not the group is Communist in nature."

http://en.wikipedia.org/wiki/Useful_idiot

4.   Bankrupt U.S. States:

"A recent study by The Center on Budget and Policy Priorities revealed that 41 states are facing severe budget shortfalls for 2009. Some states are worse off than others, with California ($31.7 billion) and Florida ($5.1 billion) leading the deficit pack. In all, the 41 states are currently facing a $71.9

billion budget shortfall. The key word here is "currently," since a similar study was conducted by the same group only three months earlier, at which time "only" 29 states were predicted to face shortfalls of a "mere" $48 billion. As the recession deepens, so will the state's budget problems, turning this "budget crisis" into a humanitarian disaster. Projections have already been made for a $200 billion shortfall by 2010."

Excerpt from the article, "41 States Face Bankruptcy in 2009" by James Sinclair, *The Free Republic*, December 7, 2008

http://www.freerepublic.com/focus/news/2144902/posts

Chapter 8

1. Biblical reference to casting the first stone:

1But Jesus went to the Mount of Olives. 2At dawn he appeared again in the temple courts, where all the people gathered around him, and he sat down to teach them. 3The teachers of the law and the Pharisees brought in a woman caught in adultery. They made her stand before the group

4and said to Jesus, "Teacher, this woman was caught in the act of adultery. 5In the Law Moses commanded us to stone such women. Now what do you say?" 6They were using this question as a trap, in order to have a basis for accusing him.

But Jesus bent down and started to write on the ground with his finger. 7When they kept on questioning him, he straightened up and said to them, "If any one of you is without sin, let him be the first to throw a stone at her." 8Again he stooped down and wrote on the ground.

9At this, those who heard began to go away one at a time, the older ones first, until only Jesus was left, with the woman still standing there. 10Jesus straightened up and asked her, "Woman, where are they? Has no one condemned you?"

11"No one, sir," she said.

"Then neither do I condemn you," Jesus declared. "Go now and leave your life of sin."

The Bible (New International Version), John 1:1-11

2.   Adolf Hitler's childhood:

"Adolf Hitler had been occasionally beaten as a child by his father and most were very intense. However, there are many other domestic (home related) issues that contributed to his adulthood behavior. His father's absence, his mother's illness, are two very important structures of behavioral outcomes. Before he became 18, his parents both were dead. There are also records of unusual (unstable) activities and acts of Adolf as a young child. The abuse that Hitler suffered from his father was only minor compared to other situations in his childhood. However, he was often beaten very viciously."

"Adolf and his father disagreed with each other when Adolf was merely of the age of 12. It was then that he began to develop his own ideas about his political views and sense of 'euphoric patriotism'. Because of this and his burning passion to become an artist, his father and Adolf's arguements became more intense, often resulting in violent outbreaks from his father."

"The abuse often consisted of beating him constantly and as a result, Adolf became more stubborn and more... 'introverted', let's say?" References in 'Mein Kampf' in the opening chapter refer to the abuse being down to alcohol on his father's account. This, however is an assumption because it is not entirely clear."

"In the light of what followed, the world witnessed Hitler's cure for the pain of being shamed. As an adult, he was constantly fearful he would appear ridiculous. He never allowed anyone to see him relaxing and playing with his dogs. His anxieties about appearing ridiculous, weak, vulnerable, incompetent, or in any way inferior are indications of this endless battle with shame. Hitler was often described by those around him as shy and avoiding eye contact, suggesting a pervasive state of shame (pp.151-152).

His anger served as a disguise for hidden shame, projecting onto the outside world the feelings of shame that were unacknowledged within. Persons who are in a state of chronic shame often avoid and deny their emotional pain by obsessive preoccupation. Hitler's obsession, the "Jewish problem" was based on his notion that the "Aryan race" was the superior one and the Jewish people were inferior. His many obsessions with superiority-inferiority, racial purity, pollution, and contamination are typical ways of bypassing feelings of shame."

Excerpt from the paper, "Child Abuse, Shame, Rage and Violence"
By Mary Katherine Armstrong, January 2001

3.   Pol Pot and children:

"The Khmer Rouge believed parents were tainted with capitalism. Consequently, children were separated from parents and brainwashed to socialism as well as taught torture methods with animals. Children were a 'dictatorial instrument of the party'and were given leadership in torture and executions."

Jackson, Karl D. (1992). *Cambodia, 1975-1978: Rendezvous with Death.* Princeton University Press. ISBN 069102541X.

4.   Cuyahoga River fire:

"On June 22, 1969, an oil slick and debris in the Cuyahoga River caught fire in Cleveland, Ohio, drawing national attention to environmental problems in Ohio and elsewhere in the United States.

This Cuyahoga River fire lasted just thirty minutes, but it did approximately fifty thousand dollars in damage — principally to some railroad bridges spanning the river. It is unclear what caused the fire, but most people believe sparks from a passing train ignited an oil slick in the Cuyahoga River. This was not the first time that the river had caught on fire. Fires occurred on the

Cuyahoga River in 1868, 1883, 1887, 1912, 1922, 1936, 1941, 1948, and in 1952. The 1952 fire caused over 1.5 million dollars in damage.

On August 1, 1969, Time magazine reported on the fire and on the condition of the Cuyahoga River. The magazine stated,

Some River! Chocolate-brown, oily, bubbling with subsurface gases, it oozes rather than flows. "Anyone who falls into the Cuyahoga does not drown," Cleveland's citizens joke grimly. "He decays". . . The Federal Water Pollution Control Administration dryly notes: "The lower Cuyahoga has no visible signs of life, not even low forms such as leeches and sludge worms that usually thrive on wastes." It is also — literally — a fire hazard."

Ohio History Central   http://www.ohiohistorycentral.org/ entry.php?rec=1642

CPSIA information can be obtained at www.ICGtesting.com
Printed in the USA
LVOW080936110911

245766LV00002B/38/P